HBR Emotional Intelligence Series

How to be human at work

The HBR Emotional Intelligence Series features smart, essential reading on the human side of professional life from the pages of *Harvard Business Review*.

Authentic Leadership	*Influence and Persuasion*
Confidence	*Leadership Presence*
Curiosity	*Managing Your Anxiety*
Dealing with Difficult People	*Mindful Listening*
Empathy	*Mindfulness*
Energy and Motivation	*Power and Impact*
Focus	*Purpose, Meaning, and Passion*
Good Habits	*Resilience*
Grit	*Self-Awareness*
Happiness	*Virtual EI*
Inclusion	

T0282914

Library of Congress Cataloging-in-Publication Data

Names: Harvard Business Review Press, issuing body.
Title: Curiosity / Harvard Business Review.
Description: Boston, Massachusetts : Harvard Business Review Press,
    [2024] | Series: Hbr emotional intelligence series | Includes index.
Identifiers: LCCN 2023051872 (print) | LCCN 2023051873 (ebook) |
    ISBN 9781647826840 (paperback) | ISBN 9781647826857 (epub)
Subjects: LCSH: Curiosity. | Emotional intelligence. | Empathy. |
    Self-consciousness (Awareness) | Compassion.
Classification: LCC BF323.C8 .C875 2024 (print) | LCC BF323.C8 (ebook) |
    DDC 152.4—dc23/eng/20240202
LC record available at https://lccn.loc.gov/2023051872
LC ebook record available at https://lccn.loc.gov/2023051873

ISBN: 978-1-64782-684-0
eISBN: 978-1-64782-685-7

Contents

1. The Five Dimensions of Curiosity   **1**

Don't ask "How curious are you?";
ask "How are you curious?"

By Todd B. Kashdan, David J. Disabato,
Fallon R. Goodman, and Carl Naughton

2. Build Your Curiosity Muscle   **15**

Five science-based recommendations.

By Tomas Chamorro-Premuzic

**3. Make Continuous Learning a Part
of Your Daily Routine**   **33**

Stay open to new discoveries.

By Helen Tupper and Sarah Ellis

Contents

4. Curiosity Is as Important as Intelligence   **51**

Enhance your ability to cope with complexity.

By Tomas Chamorro-Premuzic

5. Make Work More Meaningful   **63**

How curiosity can help you unlock your deeper purpose.

By John Coleman

6. Want Stronger Relationships at Work? Change the Way You Listen   **77**

Build trust and gain new perspectives.

By Manbir Kaur

7. How to Avoid Common Miscommunications at Work   **87**

Open up your conversation to a space of learning.

By Marsha Acker

8. How to Develop Empathy for Someone Who Annoys You   **101**

Take an interest in their perspective.

By Rebecca Knight

9. Form Stronger, Longer-Lasting Connections   113

*Lessons from a well-loved, well-networked,
and talented mathematician.*

By Utkarsh Amitabh

10. Why You Need to Cultivate Your Sense
of Wonder—Especially Now   127

*Boost your energy, inspiration, and resilience
with awe.*

By David P. Fessell and Karen Reivich

11. Four Phrases That Build a Culture of Curiosity   143

*Use them to create deeper connections
on your team.*

By Scott Shigeoka

Index   159

1

The Five Dimensions of Curiosity

By Todd B. Kashdan, David J. Disabato,
Fallon R. Goodman, and Carl Naughton

P sychologists have compiled a large body of research on the many benefits of curiosity. It enhances intelligence: In one study, highly curious children aged three to 11 improved their intelligence test scores by 12 points more than their least-curious counterparts did. It increases perseverance, or grit: Merely describing a day when you felt curious has been shown to boost mental and physical energy by 20% more than recounting a time of profound happiness. And curiosity propels us toward deeper engagement, superior performance, and more-meaningful goals: Psychology students who felt more curious than others during their first class enjoyed lectures more, got higher final grades, and subsequently enrolled in more courses in the discipline.

But in our view, another stream of research on curiosity is equally important. Since the 1950s psychologists have offered competing theories about what makes one person more curious than another. Rather than regard curiosity as a single trait, we can now break it down into five distinct dimensions. Instead of asking, "How curious are you?" we can ask, "How are you curious?" (see table 1).

A brief history

In the 1950s Daniel Berlyne was one of the first psychologists to offer a comprehensive model of curiosity. He argued that we all seek the sweet spot between two deeply uncomfortable states: *understimulation* (coping with tasks, people, or situations that lack sufficient novelty, complexity, uncertainty, or conflict) and *overstimulation*. To that end we use either what Berlyne called "diversive curiosity" (as when a bored person searches for something—*anything*—to boost arousal) or what he called "specific curiosity" (as when a hyperstimulated person tries to understand what's happening in order to reduce arousal to a more manageable level).

Building on Berlyne's insights, in 1994 George Loewenstein, of Carnegie Mellon University, proposed the "information gap" theory. He posited that people become curious upon realizing that they lack desired knowledge. This creates an aversive feeling of uncertainty, which compels them to uncover the missing information.

But these theories, focused on our inherent desire to reduce tension, don't explain other expressions of curiosity: tourists strolling through a museum, entrepreneurs poring over feedback from beta testing, people engrossed in a book. The University of Rochester's Edward Deci addressed those in the 1970s, arguing that curiosity also reflects our intrinsic motivation "to seek out novelty and challenges, to extend and exercise one's capacities, to explore, and to learn." We use it not just to avoid discomfort but to generate positive experiences.

In another body of work, the University of Delaware psychologist Marvin Zuckerman spent five decades (from the 1960s to the 2000s) studying *sensation seeking*, or the willingness to take risks to acquire varied, novel, and intense experiences. And in 2006 the psychologist Britta Renner, of the University of Konstanz, initiated the study of *social curiosity*, or people's interest in how other individuals think, feel, and behave.

The five-dimensional model

Synthesizing this and other important research, and in conjunction with our George Mason colleague

Patrick McKnight, we created a five-dimensional model of curiosity.[1] The first dimension, derived from Berlyne and Loewenstein's work, is *deprivation sensitivity*—recognizing a gap in knowledge, the filling of which offers relief. This type of curiosity doesn't necessarily feel good, but people who experience it work relentlessly to solve problems.

The second dimension, influenced by Deci's research, is *joyous exploration*—being consumed with wonder about the fascinating features of the world. This is a pleasurable state; people in it seem to possess a joie de vivre.

The third dimension, stemming from Renner's research, is *social curiosity*—talking, listening, and observing others to learn what they are thinking and doing. Human beings are inherently social animals, and the most effective and efficient way to determine whether someone is friend or foe is to gain information. Some may even snoop, eavesdrop, or gossip to do so.

TABLE 1

How are you curious?

Use this scale to indicate the degree to which the following statements describe you: 1. Does not describe me at all. 2. Barely describes me. 3. Somewhat describes me. 4. Neutral. 5. Generally describes me. 6. Mostly describes me. 7. Completely describes me.

DEPRIVATION SENSITIVITY

Thinking about solutions to difficult conceptual problems can keep me awake at night.

I can spend hours on a single problem because I just can't rest without knowing the answer.

I feel frustrated if I can't figure out the solution to a problem, so I work even harder to solve it.

I work relentlessly at problems that I feel must be solved.

It frustrates me to not have all the information I need.

Total

JOYOUS EXPLORATION

I view challenging situations as an opportunity to grow and learn.

I am always looking for experiences that challenge how I think about myself and the world.

I seek out situations where it is likely that I will have to think in depth about something.

I enjoy learning about subjects that are unfamiliar to me.

I find it fascinating to learn new information.

	Total

SOCIAL CURIOSITY

I like to learn about the habits of others.

I like finding out why people behave the way they do.

When other people are having a conversation, I like to find out what it's about.

When around other people, I like listening to their conversations.

When people quarrel, I like to know what's going on.

	Total

STRESS TOLERANCE

The smallest doubt can stop me from seeking out new experiences.

I cannot handle the stress that comes from entering uncertain situations.

I find it hard to explore new places when I lack confidence in my abilities.

I cannot function well if I am unsure whether a new experience is safe.

It is difficult to concentrate when there is a possibility that I will be taken by surprise.

	Total

(continued)

TABLE 1 *(continued)*

THRILL SEEKING

The anxiety of doing something new makes me feel excited and alive.

Risk taking is exciting to me.

When I have free time, I want to do things that are a little scary.

Creating an adventure as I go is much more appealing than a planned adventure.

I prefer friends who are excitingly unpredictable.

	Total

Scoring instructions: Compute the average score for each dimension (reverse score the items under stress tolerance). By comparing your results with those of a nationally representative sample of people in the United States, you can determine whether you are low, medium, or high on each dimension. See "What Your Score Means" to interpret your scores.

What Your Score Means

Deprivation sensitivity	Joyous exploration	Social curiosity	Stress tolerance	Thrill seeking
Low <3.7	Low <4.1	Low <3.0	Low <3.1	Low <2.6
Medium +/−4.9	Medium +/−5.2	Medium +/−4.4	Medium +/−4.4	Medium +/−3.9
High >6.0	High >6.3	High >5.8	High >5.8	High >5.2

The fourth dimension, which builds on work by Paul Silvia, a psychologist at the University of North Carolina at Greensboro, is *stress tolerance*—a willingness to accept and even harness the anxiety associated with novelty. People lacking this ability see information gaps, experience wonder, and are interested in others but are unlikely to step forward and explore.

The fifth dimension, inspired by Zuckerman, is *thrill seeking*—being willing to take physical, social, and financial risks to acquire varied, complex, and intense experiences. For people with this capacity, the anxiety of confronting novelty is something to be amplified, not reduced.

We tested this model in several ways. With Time Inc., we conducted surveys across the United States to discover which of the dimensions lead to the best outcomes and generate particular benefits. For instance, joyous exploration has the strongest link with the experience of intense positive emotions. Stress tolerance has the strongest link with satisfying the need to feel competent, autonomous, and that one belongs. Social curiosity has the strongest link with being a kind, generous, modest person.

With Merck KGaA, we explored attitudes toward and expressions of work-related curiosity. In a survey of 3,000 workers in China, Germany, and the United States, we found that 84% believe curiosity catalyzes new ideas, 74% think it inspires unique, valuable talents, and 63% think it helps one get promoted. In other studies across diverse units and geographies, we found evidence that four of the dimensions— joyous exploration, deprivation sensitivity, stress tolerance, and social curiosity—improve work outcomes. The latter two seem to be particularly important: Without the ability to tolerate stress, employees are less likely to seek challenges and resources and to voice dissent and are more likely to feel enervated and to disengage. Additionally, socially curious employees are better than others at resolving conflicts with colleagues, more likely to receive social support, and more effective at building connections, trust, and commitment on their teams. People or groups high in both dimensions are more innovative and creative.

A monolithic view of curiosity is insufficient to understand how that quality drives success and fulfillment in work and life. To discover and leverage talent and to form groups that are greater than the sum of their parts, a more nuanced approach is needed.

TODD B. KASHDAN is a professor of psychology at George Mason University who studies well-being, psychological flexibility, curiosity, courage, and resilience. He is the author of *Curious?*, *The Upside of Your Dark Side*, and *The Art of Insubordination*. DAVID J. DISABATO is a doctoral student in clinical psychology at George Mason University and a consultant with Time Inc. and Merck KGaA. FALLON R. GOODMAN is a doctoral student in clinical psychology at George Mason University and a consultant with Time Inc. and Merck KGaA. CARL NAUGHTON is a linguist and an educational scientist who consults with Merck KGaA.

Note

1. Todd B. Kashdan et al., "The Five-Dimensional Curiosity Scale: Capturing the Bandwidth of Curiosity and Identifying Four Unique Subgroups of Curious People," *Journal of Research in Personality* 73 (2018): 130–149.

Reprinted from *Harvard Business Review*,
September–October 2018 (product #S18053).

2

Build Your Curiosity Muscle

By Tomas Chamorro-Premuzic

Curiosity is best defined as the motivation to learn, be open to new ideas, and explore novel environments and situations.[1] With this meaning in mind, there are obvious reasons for one to harness and develop their curiosity.

First, curiosity is an important dimension of leadership effectiveness. If you want to manage or lead people, it helps to display curiosity, not least because this will help *them* harness their own curiosity.[2]

Second, curiosity enables the ability to keep learning—essential if you want to future-proof your career and yourself. My book *I, Human: AI, Automation, and the Quest to Reclaim What Makes Us Unique* illustrates how the skills required to keep up with our changing work environment are evolving so quickly that honing our curiosity muscle is now a survival mechanism.

Third, employers are asking for it. Curiosity is frequently listed as one of the most critical and sought-after dimensions of talent, no matter what job, industry, and seniority level.[3] For example, at ManpowerGroup, our recruiters and talent agents often hire on curiosity, which our clients appreciate. The reason is clear: While we may not know what tomorrow's jobs will be, employees' motivation and ability to upskill and reskill for those jobs will significantly increase if they're curious.[4]

So, what can you do to build and exercise your curiosity muscle?

Here are five science-based recommendations.

Ditch all excuses

Everybody wants to be curious, and few things are more intellectually fulfilling than harnessing our curiosity, whether for trivial or deep existential matters.[5] However, too many things stand in the way of unleashing our hungry minds. Common barriers include being time-deprived, having to focus on predictable tasks and deliver "sure" results, and being in boring or unstimulating work environments.[6]

Yet these are merely excuses. In reality, there's nothing actually stopping us from harnessing our curiosity. It's really just about picking the right priorities and making a deliberate effort to learn, having novel experiences, and closing the gap between what we know and want to know.[7] This is why people in the same team or company will display very different levels of curiosity, even when they're managed by the same boss.[8]

So, don't expect your manager to harness your curiosity—it's your own responsibility. For practical examples that may help you increase your workplace curiosity, consider:

- Setting aside 20 to 30 minutes per day to be intentional about cultivating curiosity, even

if it's after hours or before your work shift
starts

- Sharing ideas with colleagues, particularly
around long-term strategic issues or how
to improve existing processes and strategies

- Getting into the habit of asking why as often
as you can so that you get to the nitty-gritty
of things and start to explore things in-depth
rather than superficially

Find the right angle

One of the most obvious issues we must address
to boost our curiosity is the "what" question—that
is, I'd love to be curious, but curious about what?[9]
Unsurprisingly, it's a lot easier to display curiosity
about things we're already interested in. Identifying
your intrinsic motivation will help. In the words of
Charles Bukowski, "Find what you love and let it kill

you."[10] (OK, not literally.) Ask yourself the following questions:

- What is it you'd love to know more about?

- In what area would you love to be an expert?

- What are the questions and topics that could occupy you for ages, that make you lose track of time?

Likewise, it's important you find "white spaces"—times and places where you can avoid being distracted by work or mundane tasks and devote yourself to deep thinking.[11] In essence, identifying the right problem, and falling in love with it, equate to winning half the battle.[12] After that, your curiosity will be your fuel.

To be sure, there are many instances when discovering or nurturing curiosity about uninteresting things will also help. In such cases, the trick is to find an angle or dimension of the problem that matters more to you. For example, you may not be interested in technology, which can make working on a tech problem tedious and uninspiring. But with a little bit of thinking and exploration, you may find certain human or psychological angles that matter deeply to you that also connect to technology—how technology impacts productivity, morale, alienation, or well-being. Discovering the angle that matters turns extrinsic and mundane tasks into meaningful and useful activities and invites your curiosity to boost expertise.

Change your routine

Research shows that one of the most common habits of creative and curious individuals is that they are allergic to routine, which quickly elicits boredom and disengagement in them.[13] Injecting changes into your typical routine will create novel experiences which can trigger new ideas and questions.

Think about changing the people you work with, deal with, or see on a typical day, switching when and how you perform your daily tasks, what route you take to work, where you eat, or what you do on the weekend.[14] Even small changes to routine, such as where you place your laptop, who you go for lunch with, what virtual meetings you join (or stop joining), what new hobbies you start outside of work, can have a big impact on your mindset and curiosity.

Since the brain is fundamentally lazy, we tend to optimize our lives for familiarity and avoid novelty, which can create stress, anxiety, or more work.[15] In a new situation, you have to work out what to do, as opposed to going into autopilot.[16] Small changes to your daily routine will inject novelty and variety to your life, and even random variation can trigger your curiosity and result in novel interests.

Experiment

The main advantage of curiosity is that it's usually fun.[17] Indeed, curiosity enhances focus and concentration and creates a state of flow optimal for creativity and experimentation.[18] See this as an opportunity to try things out, combine new ideas, and ask deeper, more meaningful questions, which can transport you to unknown places and develop niche expertise.

Interestingly, advances in AI, notably generative AI, have belittled the value of human knowledge, since AI will always know more answers to more questions than any human.[19] And yet, AI still relies on humans to supply the questions or prompts. Even if, ultimately, it learns to prompt itself, AI will simply be replicating human prompts.

It's clear that one of our unique, and exclusively human, qualities is our ability to experience free-floating curiosity—curiosity that is "agentic," that comes from us, from our intuition or personal interests as well as from serendipity. Even when we know the starting point, we never quite know the end.

So, set yourself up for experimentation by going outside your comfort zone to inquire about new topics and understand stuff you've never thought about. Science shows that novelty seeking is one of the most consistent predictors of curiosity.[20] Try things out, especially if they're not obviously related to your values, preferences, and experiences. Discover the joys of new interests, guilty pleasures, and variety. And, as Harvard Business School professor Amy Edmondson notes in *Right Kind of Wrong: The Science of Failing Well*, be curious enough to learn from your errors and turn them into smart failures.

When bored, just switch

Harnessing your curiosity muscle should be a pleasant experience, more like swimming than heavy weightlifting. If you find yourself stuck, losing interest, or satiated—much like when schoolkids are forced to finish repetitive boring homework—then switch tasks and give your mind the freedom to both wonder and wander.[21] Your curiosity should propel you toward effortless learning and joyful concentration, as a wave propels a surfer or the wind propels a sailboat.

This is the difference between self-driven exploration and experimentation, which unleash your deep curiosity, and extrinsic-based learning, which tends to work against it. Instead of suppressing your genuine interests and passion for learning, let them guide you to the places you actually want to go.

A final point to consider: As with any psychological trait, curiosity is part nature, part nurture. This means that we all have a natural predisposition to be more (or less) curious, irrespective of where we are and the environment we're in. That said, there's a great deal of room for improvement. The best estimates indicate that curiosity is around 50% nature, meaning around 50% remains malleable—albeit much of that will cement in adulthood.[22] Thus, while it's unlikely someone who is naturally uncurious will suddenly achieve Einstein levels of curiosity (and vice versa), we can all strengthen or tweak whatever baseline level of curiosity we have. But, like all skills, it requires dedication.

Are you ready to flex?

TOMAS CHAMORRO-PREMUZIC is the chief innovation officer at ManpowerGroup, a professor of business psychology at University College London and Columbia University, cofounder of deepersignals.com, and an associate at Harvard's Entrepreneurial Finance Lab. He is the author of *Why Do So Many Incompetent Men Become Leaders?* (Harvard Business Review Press, 2019), on which his TEDx talk was based. His latest book is *I, Human: AI, Automation, and the Quest to Reclaim What Makes Us Unique* (Harvard Business Review Press, 2023). Find him at www.drtomas.com.

Notes

1. Celeste Kidd and Benjamin Y. Hayden, "The Psychology and Neuroscience of Curiosity," *Neuron* 88, no. 3 (2015): 449–460.
2. Timothy A. Judge et al., "Personality and Leadership: A Qualitative and Quantitative Review," *Journal of Applied Psychology* 87, no. 4 (2002): 765–780.

3. Hari Srinivasan, "The Trending Skill You Didn't Know You Needed: Curiosity," LinkedIn, May 21, 2020, https://www.linkedin.com/business/learning/blog/top-skills-and-courses/the-trending-skill-you-didn-t-know-you-needed-or-future-proof.

4. Sophie von Stumm, Benedikt Hell, and Tomas Chamorro-Premuzic, "The Hungry Mind: Intellectual Curiosity Is the Third Pillar of Academic Performance," *Perspectives on Psychological Science 6*, no. 6 (2011): 574–588.

5. Nicola S. Schutte and John M. Malouff, "Connections Between Curiosity, Flow and Creativity," *Personality and Individual Differences* 152 (2020), https://doi.org/10.1016/j.paid.2019.109555.

6. Daniel T. Willingham, "Why Aren't We Curious About the Things We Want to Be Curious About?" *New York Times*, October 18, 2019, https://www.nytimes.com/2019/10/18/opinion/sunday/curiosity-brain.html; Paul J. Silvia, "Interest—The Curious Emotion," *Current Directions in Psychological Science* 17, no. 1 (2008): 57–60; Filip Lievens et al., "Killing the Cat? A Review of Curiosity at Work," *Academy of Management Annals* 16, no. 1 (2022): 179–216.

7. Jordan Litman, Tiffany Hutchins, and Ryan Russon, "Epistemic Curiosity, Feeling-of-Knowing, and Exploratory Behaviour," *Cognition and Emotion* 19, no. 4 (2005): 559–582.

8. Todd B. Kashdan et al., "Curiosity Has Comprehensive Benefits in the Workplace: Developing and Validating a

Multidimensional Workplace Curiosity Scale in United States and German Employees," *Personality and Individual Differences* 155 (2020), https://doi.org/10.1016/j .paid.2019.109717.

9. Zhaozhen Xu et al., "What Makes Us Curious? Analysis of a Corpus of Open-Domain Questions," working paper, October 28, 2021, https://arxiv.org/abs/2110 .15409.

10. Charles Bukowski manuscripts, https://bukowski.net/ manuscripts/.

11. Regan Bach, "Creating 'White Space': The Key to Increased Creativity and Productivity," Medium, February 2, 2019, https://reganbach.medium.com/creating-white -space-the-key-to-increased-creativity-and-productivity -50af0d1c2811.

12. Nicola S. Schutte and John M. Malouff, "A Meta-Analysis of the Relationship Between Curiosity and Creativity," *Journal of Creative Behavior* 54 (2019): 940–947.

13. Vered Amit, ed., *Thinking Through Sociality: An Anthropological Interrogation of Key Concepts* (New York: Berghahn Books, 2015).

14. Tomas Chamorro-Premuzic, "Failures Can Lead to Success. Scientists Help You Predict Which Ones Will," *Fast Company*, August 25, 2023, https://www.fastcompany .com/90942289/how-to-predict-whether-failures-may -actually-lead-to-success-according-to-science.

15. Lisa Feldman Barrett, "Your Brain Is Not for Thinking," *New York Times*, November 23, 2020, https://www

.nytimes.com/2020/11/23/opinion/brain-neuroscience
-stress.html.

16. Daniel Kahneman, *Thinking, Fast and Slow* (New York:
    Farrar, Straus and Giroux, 2013).

17. Marco Lauriola et al., "Epistemic Curiosity and Self-
    Regulation," *Personality and Individual Differences* 83
    (2015): 202–207.

18. Todd B. Kashdan, Paul Rose, and Frank D. Fincham, "Cu-
    riosity and Exploration: Facilitating Positive Subjective
    Experiences and Personal Growth Opportunities," *Jour-
    nal of Personality Assessment* 82, no. 3 (2004): 291–305.

19. Tomas Chamorro-Premuzic, "How ChatGPT Is Redefin-
    ing Human Expertise: Or How to Be Smart When AI Is
    Smarter Than You," *Forbes*, January 12, 2023, https://
    www.forbes.com/sites/tomaspremuzic/2023/01/12/how
    -chatgpt-is-redefining-human-expertise-or-how-to-be
    -smart-when-ai-is-smarter-than-you/?.

20. Naomi Wentworth and Sam L. Witryol, "Curiosity, Ex-
    ploration, and Novelty-Seeking," in Marc H. Bornstein
    et al., eds., *Well-Being: Positive Development Across the
    Life Course* (Mahwah, NJ: Lawrence Erlbaum Associates
    Publishers, 2003), 281–294.

21. Tengteng Tan, Hong Zou, Chuansheng Chen,
    and Jin Luo, "Mind Wandering and the Incubation
    Effect in Insight Problem Solving," *Creativity Research
    Journal* 27, no. 4 (2015): 375–382.

22. Robert Plomin, *Blueprint: How DNA Makes Us Who
    We Are* (Cambridge, MA: MIT Press, 2018); Tomas

Chamorro-Premuzic, "If You Want to Change, Don't Read This," hbr.org, December 26, 2013, https://hbr.org/2013/12/if-you-want-to-change-dont-read-this.

Adapted from "How to Build Your Curiosity Muscle," on hbr.org, November 3, 2023 (product #H07V9C).

3

Make Continuous Learning a Part of Your Daily Routine

By Helen Tupper and Sarah Ellis

Our capacity for learning is becoming the currency we trade on in our careers. Where we once went to work to learn to do a job, learning now *is* the job. Adaptive and proactive learners are highly prized assets for organizations and when we invest in our learning, we create long-term dividends for our career development.

Reid Hoffman, the founder of LinkedIn, shared that when assessing founders of potential investments, he looks for individuals who have an "infinite learning curve": people who are constantly learning, and quickly.[1] Satya Nadella, the CEO of Microsoft, echoed the importance of learning when he said, "The learn-it-all will always do better than the know-it-all."[2]

However, it's not as simple as just acquiring new knowledge. In our increasingly "squiggly" careers, where people change roles more frequently and fluidly and develop in different directions, the ability to unlearn, learn, and relearn is vital for long-term success. Based on our experience designing and delivering career development training for over 50,000 people worldwide, working with organizations including Microsoft, Virgin, and Levi's, we've identified several techniques and tools to help you make continuous learning part of your day-to-day development.

Learning

As we spend so much of our time, energy, and effort at our day jobs, they provide the most significant opportunities for learning. The challenge is that we don't invest intentionally in everyday development—we're so busy with tasks and getting the job done that there's no space left for anything else. Deprioritizing our development is a risky career strategy because it reduces our resilience and ability to respond to the changes happening around us.

Here are three ways to take ownership of your learning at work.

Learn from others

The people you spend time with are a significant source of knowledge. Creating a diverse learning community will offer you new perspectives and reduce the risk that you'll end up in an echo chamber. Set a goal of having one *curiosity coffee* each month, virtually or in person, with someone you haven't met before. This could be someone in a different department who could help you view your organization through a new lens or someone in your profession at another company who could broaden your knowledge. Extend your curiosity even further by ending each conversation with the question: "Who else do you think it would be useful for me to connect with?" Not only does this create the chance for new connections, but you might also benefit from a direct introduction.

Experiment

Experiments help you test, learn, and adapt along the way. There are endless ways you can experiment at work—for example, using different tools to increase the interactivity of your virtual and hybrid meetings, rearranging your meetings to increase engagement and productivity, or even trying out new negotiation tactics.

For an experiment to be effective, it needs to be a conscious choice and labeled as an opportunity for learning. Keep a *learn-fast log* where you track the experiments you're running and what you're learning. It's important to remember that you should expect some experiments to fail, as that's the nature of exploring the unknown.

Create a collective curriculum

In a squiggly career, everyone's a learner and everyone's a teacher. As a team, consider how you can create a collective curriculum where you're learning from and with each other. We've seen organizations effectively use *skills swaps,* where individuals share one skill they're happy to help other people learn. This could look like a creative problem-solver offering to share the processes and tools they find most helpful, or someone who has expertise in coding running beginner lunch-and-learn sessions. Skills swaps are a good example of democratized development, where everyone has something to contribute and is learning continually.

Unlearning

Unlearning means letting go of the safe and familiar and replacing it with something new and unknown. Skills and behaviors that helped you get to where you are can hold you back from getting to where you want to be. For example, a leader might need to unlearn their default of always being the person who speaks first in meetings. Or a first-time manager might need to unlearn always saying yes as their workload increases. Whether you're new to the workforce or have decades of experience, unlearning can feel uncomfortable. But we're all more adaptable than we give ourselves credit for.

Here are three ways to make unlearning an active part of how you work.

Connect with challengers

We unlearn when we look at a problem or opportunity through a new lens. This is more likely to happen if we're spending time with people who challenge us and think differently than we do. The purpose of connecting with challengers is not to agree or debate but to listen and consider: What can I learn from this person?

Seek out people who have an *opposite experience* from you in some way. For example, if you're in a large organization, find someone who has only ever worked for themselves. If you have 25 years of experience, find someone just starting out. People who have made different choices and have different areas of expertise than you are a good place to discover a new source of challenge. Asking people, "How would you approach this challenge?" or "What has your experience of this situation been?" is a good way to explore an alternative point of view.

Identify habits and holdbacks

We all have habits that helped us get to where we are today. However, habits can create blind spots that stop us from seeing different ways of doing things or new approaches to try out. Our brains use habits to create mental shortcuts that might make us miss opportunities to reflect on and unlearn our automatic responses.

Changing habits is hard. To make progress, identify *one habit holdback* that you have. This is something you do by default every week at work and your hypothesis is that it's holding you back in some way, perhaps because it's time-consuming or you spot that your learning has stalled in an area. It could be a small habit, such as being the person who always sets the agenda for a meeting. It could be something more significant, such as being the person who solves other people's problems. Your job is to let go of that habit and try something new. For example, if you're the person who usually sets the meeting agenda, ask for volunteers to take on that task for the next three months. If you habitually jump to problem-solving, you could try asking open questions like, "What ideas do you have?" or "What have you tried so far?"

Ask propelling questions

Propelling questions reset our status quo and encourage us to explore different ways of doing things. They often start with: How might we? How could I? What would happen if? These questions are designed to prevent our existing knowledge from limiting our ability to imagine new possibilities. They fast-forward us into the future and prompt positive action in the present.

To put propelling questions into practice, it's helpful to pair up with someone else and take turns asking and answering questions. These five peer-to-peer propelling questions can get you started.

1. Imagine it's ten years from now. What three significant changes have happened in your industry?

2. How might you divide your role between you and a robot/AI?

3. Which of your strengths would be most useful if your organization doubled in size?

4. How could you transfer your talents if your industry disappeared overnight?

5. If you were rebuilding this business tomorrow, what would you do differently?

Relearning

Relearning is recognizing that how we apply our strengths is always changing and that our potential is always a work in progress. We need to regularly reassess our abilities and how they need to be adapted for our current context. For example, collaboration remains as important as ever, but maybe you're re-learning how to do it in a hybrid world of work. Or maybe you've made a career change and you're re-learning what it looks like to transfer your talents to a new setting.

Here are three ways to use relearning to stay nimble in the face of change.

Stretch your strengths

One of the ways to make your strengths stronger is to use them in as many different situations as possible. If you become too comfortable applying them in the same way, your development stalls. *Strengths solving* involves relearning how to use your strengths to offer support and solve problems outside of your day-to-day work. This could be in your networks, organizations you volunteer for, or even side projects you're involved in. For example, one of our workshop participants is a commercial marketing director who applies her creativity not only to her day job, but also to the successful brownie business she created during the pandemic.

Get fresh-eyed feedback

Looking at your skills from someone else's perspective will help you identify opportunities to relearn. Asking for feedback can help open your eyes to your development blind spots and take back control of your growth. When your objective is to relearn, we find that presenting people with *even better questions* works particularly well in providing them with the safety to share candid feedback. For example: How could I make my presentations even better? How could I make our team meetings even better? What's one way I could do an even better job of progressing my performance?

Relearn resilience

Relearning takes resilience, and if you feel pessimistic about the progress you're making, you might be tempted to give up. Refocusing on what's working well can help you continue to move forward.

Try writing down three *very small successes* at the end of each day for two weeks. Your successes can come from your personal or professional life, and though it can be hard to spot them at first, the more you do this, the easier it gets. A very small success could include asking one person for feedback, helping a colleague prepare for a presentation, taking a lunch break, or cooking a new dish for the first time. At the end of two weeks, you'll have 42 very small successes, creating the motivation and momentum to continue investing in your development, even when it feels hard.

We can't predict how our careers will develop or what the world of work will look like in the future, but we can take steps to become more adaptable. Investing in our ability to learn, unlearn, and relearn helps us increase our readiness for the opportunities that change presents and our resilience to the inevitable challenges we'll experience along the way.

HELEN TUPPER and SARAH ELLIS are the founders of Amazing If, an award-winning company with a mission to make squiggly careers better for everyone. Together they are the authors of two *Sunday Times* bestsellers, *The Squiggly Career* and *You Coach You*. Their TEDx talk, "The Best Career Path Isn't Always a Straight Line," has been watched by almost two million people and their weekly *Squiggly Careers* podcast has had more than four million downloads. Amazing If works with organizations, including Microsoft, Levi's, BBC, Danone, and Visa, to support people with the skills to succeed in a squiggly career.

Prior to Amazing If, Sarah's career included leadership roles at Barclays and Sainsbury's before becoming managing director at creative agency Gravity Road. Sarah is an alumnus of Harvard, London, and Warwick Business Schools (MBA), a qualified professional coach, and a mental health first aider. She is also cochair of the Mayor of London Workspace Advisory Board. Sarah lives in London with her partner and her bug-loving six-year-old, Max. You can follow her on LinkedIn and find free career development tools at www.amazingif.com.

Prior to Amazing If, Helen held leadership roles for Microsoft, Virgin, and BP and was awarded the FT & 30% Club's Women in Leadership MBA Scholarship. In 2023 Helen was awarded a place on EY's International Winning Women program. She is mum to Henry and Madeleine. You can follow her on LinkedIn and find free career development tools at www.amazingif.com.

Notes

1. Adam Bryant, "What Reid Hoffman Wants in a Founder: 'An Infinite Learning Curve,'" CNBC, November 5, 2018, https://www.cnbc.com/2018/11/04/what-reid-hoffman -wants-in-a-founder-an-infinite-learning-curve.html.
2. Jessi Hempel, "Satya Nadella on Growth Mindsets: 'The Learn-It-All Does Better Than the Know-It-All,'" LinkedIn, December 9, 2019, https://www.linkedin.com/pulse/ satya-nadella-growth-mindsets-learn-it-all-does-better -jessi-hempel/.

Adapted from "Make Learning a Part of Your Daily Routine," on hbr.org, November 4, 2021 (product #H06OF5).

4

Curiosity Is as Important as Intelligence

By Tomas Chamorro-Premuzic

There seems to be wide support for the idea that we're living in an "age of complexity," which implies that the world has never been more intricate. This idea is based on the rapid pace of technological changes and the vast amount of information that we're generating (the two are related). Consider the philosophers Leibniz (17th century) and Diderot (18th century), who were already complaining about information overload. The "horrible mass of books" they referenced represented only a tiny portion of what we know today, and yet much of what we know today will be equally insignificant to future generations.[1]

In any event, the relative complexity of different eras matters little to the person simply struggling to cope with it in everyday life. Perhaps, then, the right question is not "Is this era more complex?" but "Why are some people more able to manage complexity?" Although complexity is context-dependent, it's also determined by a person's disposition. The three key psychological qualities that enhance our ability to manage complexity are: *IQ, EQ,* and *CQ.*

IQ

As most people know, IQ stands for *intelligence quotient* and refers to mental ability. What fewer people know, or like to accept, is that IQ *does* affect a wide range of real-world outcomes, such as job performance and objective career success.[2] The main reason is that higher levels of IQ enable people to learn and solve novel problems faster. At face value, IQ tests seem quite abstract, mathematical, and disconnected from everyday problems. Yet they're a powerful tool to predict our ability to manage complexity. In fact, IQ is a much stronger predictor of performance on complex tasks than on simple ones.[3]

Complex environments are richer in information, which creates more cognitive load and demands more brainpower or deliberate thinking from us; we cannot navigate them in autopilot (or Kahneman's System 1 thinking).[4] IQ is a measure of that brainpower, as megabytes or processing speed are a measure of the operations a computer can perform—and at what speed. Unsurprisingly, there's a substantial correlation between IQ and *working memory*, our mental capacity for handling multiple pieces of temporary information at once.[5] Try memorizing a phone number while asking someone for directions and remembering your shopping list, and you'll get a good sense of your IQ. (Research shows that working memory training does not enhance our long-term ability to deal with complexity, though some evidence suggests it delays mental decline in older people, as per the "use it or lose it" theory.[6])

EQ

EQ stands for *emotional quotient* and concerns our ability to perceive, control, and express emotions. EQ relates to complexity management in three main ways. First, individuals with higher EQ are less susceptible to stress and anxiety.[7] Since complex situations are resourceful and demanding, they're likely to induce pressure and stress. But high EQ acts as a buffer. Second, EQ is a key ingredient of interpersonal skills, which means that people with higher EQ are better equipped to navigate complex organizational politics and advance in their careers.[8] Even in today's hyperconnected world, what most employers look for is not technical expertise, but soft skills, especially when it comes to management and leadership roles.[9] Third, people with higher EQ tend to be more entrepreneurial, meaning they're more proactive at exploiting opportunities, taking risks, and turning creative ideas into actual innovations.[10] All this makes EQ an important quality for adapting to uncertain, unpredictable, and complex environments.

CQ

CQ stands for *curiosity quotient* and concerns having a hungry mind.[11] People with higher CQ are more inquisitive and open to new experiences. They find novelty exciting and are quickly bored with routine. They tend to generate many original ideas and are counterconformist. CQ hasn't been as deeply studied as EQ and IQ, but there's evidence to suggest it's just as important when it comes to managing complexity in two major ways. First, individuals with higher CQ are generally more tolerant of ambiguity.[12] This nuanced, sophisticated, subtle thinking style defines the very essence of complexity. Second, CQ leads to higher levels of intellectual investment and knowledge acquisition over time, especially in formal domains of education, such as science and art (this is different from IQ's measurement of raw intellectual horsepower).[13] Knowledge and expertise, much like experience, translate complex situations into familiar ones. Thus, CQ is the ultimate tool to produce simple solutions for complex problems.

Although IQ is hard to coach, EQ and CQ can be developed. As Albert Einstein famously said, "I have no special talents. I am only passionately curious."

TOMAS CHAMORRO-PREMUZIC is the chief innovation officer at ManpowerGroup, a professor of business psychology at University College London and Columbia University, cofounder of deepersignals.com, and an associate at Harvard's Entrepreneurial Finance Lab. He is the author of *Why Do So*

Many Incompetent Men Become Leaders? (Harvard Business Review Press, 2019), on which his TEDx talk was based. His latest book is *I, Human: AI, Automation, and the Quest to Reclaim What Makes Us Unique* (Harvard Business Review Press, 2023). Find him at www.drtomas.com.

Notes

1. Daniel Rosenberg, "Introduction: Early Modern Information Overload," *Journal of the History of Ideas* 64, no. 1 (2003): 1–9.
2. Nathan R. Kuncel, Deniz S. Ones, and Paul R. Sackett, "Individual Differences as Predictors of Work, Educational, and Broad Life Outcomes," *Personality and Individual Differences* 49, no. 4 (2010): 331–336; Thomas W. H. Ng et al., "Predictors of Objective and Subjective Career Success: A Meta-Analysis," *Personnel Psychology* 58, no. 2 (2005): 367–408.
3. Linda S. Gottfredson, "Why G Matters: The Complexity of Everyday Life," *Intelligence* 24, no. 1 (1997): 79–132.
4. Nilli Lavie et al., "Load Theory of Selective Attention and Cognitive Control," *Journal of Experimental Psychology: General* 133, no. 3 (2004): 339–354.
5. Roberto Colom et al., "Working Memory and Intelligence Are Highly Related Constructs, but Why?" *Intelligence* 36 (2008): 584–606.

6. Monica Melby-Lervåg and Charles Hulme, "Is Working Memory Training Effective? A Meta-Analytic Review," *Developmental Psychology* 49, no. 2 (2013): 270–291; Martin Buschkuehl et al., "Impact of Working Memory Training on Memory Performance in Old-Old Adults," *Psychology and Aging* 23, no. 4 (2008): 743–753.

7. Moïra Mikolajczak, Clémentine Menil, and Olivier Luminet, "Explaining the Protective Effect of Trait Emotional Intelligence Regarding Occupational Stress: Exploration of Emotional Labour Processes," *Journal of Research in Personality* 41, no. 5 (2007): 1107–1117.

8. Tomas Chamorro-Premuzic, *The Talent Delusion: Why Data, Not Intuition, Is the Key to Unlocking Human Potential* (London: Piatkus, 2017).

9. Tomas Chamorro-Premuzic, "5 Ways to Develop Talent for an Unpredictable Future," hbr.org, October 9, 2023, https://hbr.org/2023/10/5-ways-to-develop-talent-for-an-unpredictable-future.

10. Franziska Leutner et al., "The Relationship Between the Entrepreneurial Personality and the Big Five Personality Traits," *Personality and Individual Differences* 63 (2014): 58–63.

11. Sophie von Stumm, Benedikt Hell, and Tomas Chamorro-Premuzic, "The Hungry Mind: Intellectual Curiosity Is the Third Pillar of Academic Performance," *Perspectives on Psychological Science* 6, no. 6 (2011): 574–588.

12. Erica Briscoe and Jacob Feldman, "Conceptual Complexity and the Bias/Variance Tradeoff," *Cognition* 118, no. 1 (2011): 2–16.
13. Sophie von Stumm and Phillip L. Ackerman, "Investment and Intellect: A Review and Meta-Analysis," *Psychological Bulletin* 139, no. 4 (2013): 841–869.

Adapted from content posted on hbr.org,
August 27, 2014 (product #H00YMR).

5

Make Work More Meaningful

By John Coleman

Curiosity is critical to professional success. A curious mind will spot and solve problems while being unafraid to try something new. It will seek out the insights of others and open itself to expanded thinking. A curious person will never succumb to apathy, instead pushing consistently for growth, innovation, and improvement. Anyone seeking to build a successful career must embrace curiosity.

Curiosity isn't just essential to professional advancement—it's central to crafting purpose and meaning at work. We all want to feel that our work is meaningful, and we all have an opportunity to make it so. But it takes curiosity—about ourselves, our work, and the people we work with—to unlock deeper purpose each day.

In my book the *HBR Guide to Crafting Your Purpose*, I outline four essential ways in which any person can better pursue professional purpose: craft your work, make work a craft, connect work to service, and invest in positive relationships. Engaging in these four simple practices makes any job more meaningful. But each of us must embrace curiosity to fully mine these practices for meaning.

Craft your work

One of the best ways to enhance the meaning you get from work is through job crafting—the art of making small changes to your work life to turn the job you have into the job you want. The idea is that, by making small changes, you can tailor your work to your unique passions, personality, and interests in a way that maximizes its meaning to you and others.

My favorite example is Curtis Jenkins, a Dallas bus driver who managed to revolutionize his position by creating what reporters called a "yellow bus utopia" while changing hundreds of lives.

Curiosity is a necessary precondition for job crafting. It starts with a self-evaluation. Ask yourself questions such as, What am I good at (really)? What do I love to do? What makes me happy on the job? A thoughtful self-understanding explored deeply and with an open mind can provide the foundation upon which job crafting is built.

Next, apply this self-awareness to the job:

- What elements of my job could I tweak to be more meaningful for me and more impactful for others?

- Can what I currently do be done differently?

- Is my job, as structured, solving the most important problems—for both the organization and those it serves—in the best ways?

To get started, list the core people you serve and the outcomes of your job that help serve them well. Then reflect on your current tasks and see if there are ways to serve those people as well or better by doing things differently. You may find ways to craft your work that are both better for them and more meaningful for you.

Make work a craft

The second way to make work more meaningful is to make it a craft. For much of history, people practiced professions intergenerationally. Trades like farming, carpentry, and cobblery might be passed down generation to generation in a family; a person would painstakingly perfect their craft over a lifetime. This quest for perfection and constant improvement created the most memorable achievements in history—from the frescoes of the Sistine Chapel to breakthroughs in genetics and the elegant simplicity of the original Mac.

This commitment to craftsmanship offers a sense of purpose in and of itself. As I explain in my book, we all gain meaning from work well done. There's intrinsic motivation and purpose in knowing that we've put our best efforts into something, that we've honed a craft in a way that challenges us.

But how can we find opportunities for craft in our modern jobs? After all, building financial models or leading a team in a factory can feel a bit distant from Michelangelo's masterworks or the genius of Steve Jobs. But craft is not about historical impact. It's about self-improvement and a quest to push the limits of our own performance—to take on new challenges and achieve something hard and unique. When I was an analyst at McKinsey, this looked like building beautiful Excel models with elegant formulas that could last clients years. I did this whether the partners noticed or not because I took pride in challenging and improving myself. In your job, it's something else. Curiosity can unlock it.

Ask yourself:

- What are the core elements of my job that require excellence?

- What skills do I need to perform that job well?

- What are one or two areas I can focus on now to make a craft, and how can I improve day by day until I do those things better than anyone else and to the best of my ability?

To begin, pick one area of your work you'd like to try to hone and perfect. Choose something you enjoy and that's important to your job. Assess the five to 10 ways you could make it better, then start to implement those improvements and challenge yourself. Keep daily notes or save old versions sequentially so that you can see your improvement over time.

Connect work to service

There's almost nothing in life that improves our sense of well-being and purpose like service to others. Numerous studies have shown that acts of service have an immediate impact on happiness and fulfillment.[1] In my own life, I've rarely felt as purposeful as when building a Habitat for Humanity home with colleagues, serving in a soup kitchen, or reading to kids at a local school.

Service doesn't have to be confined to volunteering in a community, however. In any job, there are at least six opportunities to serve others: clients or customers, colleagues, capital, community, partners, and people we love. Knowing this and seeking opportunities for service in each of these areas can bring meaning to work.

Identifying the people we serve and ways to serve them requires deep-seated curiosity. Consider these questions:

- Who are my clients?

- What do they need?

- What are the key obstacles to their well-being that I'm helping to overcome, and how can I do better?

- Which colleagues most need my help?

- How can I effectively offer that help without expectation of return?

- Which two or three people could I best serve today?

These questions, founded in curiosity, are at the heart of service to others. Pick two of the six areas you like—colleagues and customers, for example.

Think of two to three individuals in each of those two groups whom you could better serve. Then spend the next month trying to really understand them and how your work can serve them well.

Invest in positive relationships

In social science literature, perhaps nothing is as central to happiness as meaningful, positive relationships. They are essential to Martin Seligman's PERMA framework for flourishing, and also to the finding of the Harvard Grant Study that "happiness is love."[2] Other studies echo these findings.

Relationships aren't just confined to our personal lives. Each workday we spend more than eight hours with colleagues, whether remotely or in person. And trying to navigate work in the absence of meaningful relationships is a recipe for disappointment. Positive professional relationships can help us flourish, make others happy, and create extraordinary corporate cultures.

At work, as at home, relationships rest on empathy and curiosity.[3] We can't have a relationship of mutual care and respect with someone if we don't display a genuine curiosity for them. Ask:

- Who are they?

- What matters to them?

- What are their anxieties and fears, passions, and purpose?

- On any given day, how are they feeling?

- What are they interested in intellectually?

Approaching others with curiosity will naturally build your own empathy and show that you care, creating meaningful relationships in the process. When you're interacting with colleagues over the next month or two, consciously make a game of trying to know them better. Ask more questions than you answer. And carve out time for conversations and interactions that don't just accomplish your work tasks but also (in a professional way) enhance your relationships. Improving these work relationships will make you and those around you happier and probably make you more productive as well.

Curiosity is undoubtedly essential to professional success and is at the heart of purpose. Living with greater curiosity at work can help us craft jobs and professional environments in which we and others can flourish.

JOHN COLEMAN is the author of the *HBR Guide to Crafting Your Purpose* (Harvard Business Review Press, 2022). Subscribe to his free newsletter, *On Purpose*, follow him on social @johnwcoleman, or contact him at johnwilliamcoleman.com.

Notes

1. Gleb Tsipursky, "Is Serving Others the Key to Meaning and Purpose?" *Psychology Today*, July 14, 2016, https://www.psychologytoday.com/us/blog/intentional-insights/201607/is-serving-others-the-key-meaning-and-purpose.

2. Melissa Madeson, "Seligman's PERMA+ Model Explained: A Theory of Wellbeing," *Positive Psychology*, February 24, 2017, https://positivepsychology.com/perma-model/; Scott Stossel, "What Makes Us Happy, Revisited: A New Look at the Famous Harvard Study of What Makes People Thrive," *Atlantic*, May 2013, https://www.theatlantic.com/magazine/archive/2013/05/thanks-mom/309287.

3. Andrea Brandt, "The Secret to a Happy Relationship Is Empathy," *Psychology Today*, March 3, 2020, https://www.psychologytoday.com/us/blog/mindful-anger/202003/the-secret-happy-relationship-is-empathy.

Adapted from "4 Ways to Make Work More Meaningful," on hbr.org, October 2, 2023 (product #H07TE7).

6

Want Stronger Relationships at Work? Change the Way You Listen

By Manbir Kaur

Roan walked into the office listening to his favorite morning mix. As he got closer to his desk, his manager, Andy, intercepted him. Roan removed one of his earplugs. "There's a problem with the report you submitted yesterday. I think it needs to be worked on again. Could you get to it ASAP?"

"Was that really the first thing Andy could say to me this morning?" Roan thought.

With half his mind on the morning mix and the other half trying to listen to Andy, Roan shook his head without a word and walked on.

"Was he even listening?" wondered Andy. He was a little offended.

A lot happens in the brain during a conversation. The late Judith Glaser, author of *Conversational Intelligence*, tells us that our brain takes just 0.07 seconds in a conversation to form an initial impression of the other person's intent—whether we're going to trust them or not. Our response is then influenced by that impression. Andy and Roan's conversation can only be termed "poor."

Simplifying the neurochemistry of listening

In her book, Glaser quoted multiple researchers to explain that when we sense threat in a conversation, the amygdala (part of the limbic system in our brain) triggers the protection mode. This releases a few hormones, including cortisol. When cortisol rules over our bodies, we may not be able to engage and connect, and we're likely to become more reactive, emotional, and impulsive. We're also more likely to perceive situations negatively.

On the other hand, conversations that encourage co-operation and understanding release a different set of hormones, including oxytocin, which reinforce a bonding experience. When that happens, we stop being protective and instead begin to connect with others and build lasting relationships based on mutual trust.

By choosing the way we listen, we have the power to influence the neurochemical reactions that happen in the brain.

How we listen

Glaser's framework on conversational intelligence indicates that we listen with three prominent attitudes. Each one affects how the speaker is going to respond to us.

Listening to protect: You're on the defensive. You're trying to protect your identity and space. The speaker may feel ignored.

Listening to accept or reject: You're listening with an intent to judge. The speaker may feel labeled. You'll often see examples of this in a team meeting.

Listening to cocreate: You're listening to connect with the other person. It's psychologically safe. You approach with the intent to explore and understand:

- What are they trying to say?

- What are they thinking?

- What are they expecting to explore together?

- How can I connect to their world?

When you choose to listen with openness, the neurochemistry of your body and that of the other person will come to your aid, helping to build greater understanding.

In fact, listening is fun. It can give you new perspectives, and some curious ones, too!

How to be a good listener

Become a better listener by practicing these four tips in your next conversation:

Go in with the right intention. When you're having a conversation, go in with the intention to listen to the other person. Make sure you believe they have something of value to say—and that it's important for you to give them the chance to say it.

If Roan had immediately removed both earplugs, Andy wouldn't have felt ignored.

Instead of blaming Roan for the error, Andy could have set the context and asked if any of his instructions were unclear—a possible reason for Roan's incomplete report.

Use both your head and heart. Try to understand not just the "what" but also the "why." Good listening will

83

help you understand not just the reasons, but also help you connect with the emotions behind what's being said.

Roan could have acknowledged the mistake: "I'm sorry this didn't meet your expectations. Please help me understand how I can make the report better." Expressing and acknowledging the feelings clearly could have set the stage for a stronger conversation and helped build trust between them.

Instead of ambushing Roan right as he walked in, Andy could have been more sensitive: "I'm sorry for catching you now as I see you're just getting into work, but this is really urgent. Do you have a minute?"

Put yourself in the other person's shoes. No one understands your situation and challenges, right? Well, the other person might think the same thing. So even if you can't help because of your own constraints, listen with empathy and compassion. It's the least you can do.

Roan could have understood the urgency behind Andy's request and reassured him that he'd get to it as soon as possible: "Of course, I understand the client needs the report urgently. I'll see what can be done to make it better at the earliest."

If Roan didn't do the report right, maybe the instructions weren't clear. Andy could have spent a little time trying to explain the specifics of what was wrong: "I know you worked hard on the report, but it's not what the client wants. Maybe my instructions weren't clear. Let me know if I can help you with additional information."

Show you're engaged. Give the conversation your full attention. Ask open-ended questions in order to better understand things.

Roan should have been curious as to how he might have improved the report. Questions like, "I may need help. Could you give me more information so I can make the report stronger? What did the client not like about the report?" could have served the purpose.

———————

Try these tips for the next few conversations you have and experience how you're able to develop personal relationships with deeper connections. The more actively you listen, the more you'll be heard.

MANBIR KAUR is an executive coach (ICF-PCC) and a conversational intelligence (C-IQ) enhanced skills practitioner. She is the author of *Get Your Next Promotion* and *Are You the Leader You Want to Be?* (one of five books nominated for the C.K. Prahalad Best Business Book Award 2019).

Adapted from content posted on hbr.org, July 17, 2020.

7

How to Avoid Common Miscommunications at Work

By Marsha Acker

D o you ever feel like you're having the same conversations over and over again at work? Chances are, you're experiencing a breakdown in communication.

While we all know that clear communication is needed to successfully collaborate with our managers and team members, it's often one of the most difficult skills to master for someone new to the workforce. Why? Because many of us tend to assume that other people see and experience things the same way we do.[1]

Researcher and systems psychologist David Kantor offers a key principle that can help us overcome this bias in our thinking.[2] He came up with a theory known as *structural dynamics*, which describes how face-to-face communication works (and doesn't) and aims to help us see and understand the patterns, behaviors, and dynamics that impact our interpersonal and group conversations. According to Kantor, there's a visible and an invisible reality present in every interaction we have. To have more effective conversations based on mutual understanding, we need to learn how to navigate both.

The visible reality is the conversation we're having out loud, or the actual words that are being said. This is what most people think about when they hear the word "conversation." The invisible reality includes all the internal narratives and preconceived ideas that shape how each participant is processing the meaning and intention behind the words spoken.

The invisible reality is where things tend to go sideways. Because we instinctually assume that others see and experience things the same way we do, we tend to believe our interpretations of the conversations we engage in are correct. The issue occurs when we walk away on a different page from our manager, team, or peer, and end up digressing instead of reaching the outcome we want.

To move beyond our assumptions and get on the same page as our colleagues, we need to develop our ability to make our thinking and assumptions more visible to the person we're speaking with. We also need to look for opportunities to learn more about their thinking and assumptions. You've likely heard of this skill before. It's called *reading the room* and it's a communication superpower.

If you can learn to make the "invisible" more "visible" in your conversations at work, you'll be able to leapfrog over those annoying surface-level miscommunications and collaborate more productively with everyone. You may even be able to have conversations just once.

Below are three practices that will allow you to better read the room. You can start implementing them today.

Step 1: Focus on "how" instead of "what"

In any conversation, there will be two parallel threads happening simultaneously. The first is the "what." This is the content (or the topic) of the conversation. It's what you and the other person, or people, are talking about.

The second thread is the "how." This is how you're talking with one another—the way you're engaging together, the kinds of language being used, and the spoken or unspoken rules about whose voice holds more power in the interaction. Each of these elements is determined by your and the other person's preconceived assumptions, preferences, and behavioral tendencies, and how they come into contact during a conversation—no matter the topic.

When holding conversations with others, we tend to focus on the what. After all, addressing the topic is probably why we've come together in the first place. But to have more effective conversations about any topic, the first step is to commit to focusing on the how—because that's the part of the conversation that's less obvious, or invisible.

When things start feeling sticky in a conversation, it's time to immediately take a step back, take a breath, and make some simple observations about how the conversation is unfolding. Ask yourself: Who is speaking and who is not? Who is asking questions? Who is making assertions? What am I experiencing? What am I thinking but not saying?

When you make these observations, you've taken the first step to uncovering the dynamics at play in the conversation, simply by observing how the conversation is unfolding rather than focusing on what topic is on the table.

The next step is to begin exploring what invisible realities might be in play so that you can each engage with more clarity and empathy.

Step 2: Voice your observations

Once you've taken a step back to consider the dynamic of a conversation, you can create a "pause" by making a neutral observation aloud. This is a way to slow the interaction down and create more space for everyone to get on the same page.

In his book *Reading the Room*, David Kantor calls this a *bystand*—an effective way to begin surfacing some of the invisible realities that are affecting your conversation. When we voice what we're observing, it invites the other participant(s) to share more about what's happening for them and offer a perspective that may shift the direction of the interaction.

Importantly, a bystand should be offered from a space of neutrality and grace to avoid taking an accusatory tone. Start by stating something that you see ("I'm noticing") and then share your observation.

For example, you might say, "I'm noticing that we're not hearing from all the voices in the room." Or, "I'm noticing that the tension levels in this conversation are really high." These are both neutral comments reflecting what you're seeing.

Your bystand should then be followed by an invitation. This can come in the form of a question, like, "How are you experiencing our dynamic?" Or, "I'm wondering if anyone else is seeing something different." The goal is to encourage others to voice what's happening for them.

More often than not, a bystand of this sort—a neutral observation followed by an invitation to dialogue—will not only shift the dynamic of the conversation but will nudge participants to share critical information about how they're experiencing the moment. This practice can help you and your team avoid the kinds of miscommunications and frustrations that come from assuming you're all on the same page.

Step 3: Get curious

Now that you're focusing on the dynamics of the conversation from a place of openness rather than assumption, you're in a better position to understand what's happening for both you and the other participant(s). You can actively surface the other person's invisible realities by getting curious and making your invitation (following your bystand) even more specific.

Consider these different scenarios:

> If someone is not contributing their voice,
> gently share this observation, and then ask
> if they see something that's missing from the
> conversation. Perhaps they'll voice an opinion,
> or perhaps they'll offer additional informa-
> tion that will move the conversation in a new
> direction.

If someone seems frustrated, draw attention to the feeling and then try asking, "What's happening for you right now?" In this way, you're inviting the person to add new and helpful information to the conversation—and it may shift the dynamic from tense to productive.

If someone is constantly pushing back on the ideas that others are putting forward, name it and then ask, "What ideas have you heard from others that you support or align with?" Many times, people remain silent when they agree with an idea. Asking this question can create more space for alignment between you and the other person, allowing the ideas you agree upon to get more airtime.

In each of these examples, getting curious about your observations opens up the conversation to a space of learning. By asking questions, you learn more about where the other person is coming from and create opportunities for additional information to arise—both of which are critical for getting sticky conversations unstuck.

———————

In conversations, it's easy to feel misunderstood. It's also easy to misunderstand. (As Stephen Covey says, "We judge ourselves by our intentions and others by their behavior.") By paying attention to how communication is happening, you can make the invisible more visible. This will lead to more productive conversations with less blame, confusion, frustration, and antagonism. Invite curiosity into the room—both toward yourself and others—and you'll find it much easier to communicate clearly and see the outcomes you want.

MARSHA ACKER is the author of *Build Your Model for Leading Change: A Guided Workbook to Catalyze Clarity and Confidence in Leading Yourself and Others.* She is the founder and CEO of TeamCatapult, a leadership development firm that equips leaders at all levels to facilitate and lead sustainable behavioral change.

Notes

1. Gwendolyn Seidman, "Why Do We Like People Who Are Similar to Us?" *Psychology Today*, December 18, 2018, https://www.psychologytoday.com/us/blog/close-encounters/201812/why-do-we-people-who-are-similar-us.
2. David Kantor, *Reading the Room: Group Dynamics for Coaches and Leaders* (New York: Jossey-Bass, 2012).

Adapted from content posted on hbr.org, August 11, 2023.

8

How to Develop Empathy for Someone Who Annoys You

By Rebecca Knight

When someone you work with annoys you, it's tempting to avoid that person as much as possible. But this isn't always feasible and often only makes the situation worse. You're better off cultivating some empathy. How can you do that with a colleague who rubs you the wrong way? How can you foster curiosity instead of animosity?

What the experts say

"We've all encountered someone in the workplace who irritates us," says Annie McKee, author of *How to Be Happy at Work*, and a senior fellow at the University of Pennsylvania. "It may have to do with this person's communication style, or maybe he engages in behaviors that you find rude—he's always late to meetings, say." But at a time when work is ever more team-oriented and projects often require intense collaboration, "you have to find a way to connect and build a bridge" with even the most irritating people. Cultivating compassion for these kinds of colleagues, however trying they may be, is a good place to start, according to Rich Fernandez, CEO of Search Inside Yourself Leadership Institute. "Using empathy, you can maintain a balanced and well-calibrated approach to working with difficult people," he says. Here are some pointers.

Reflect

For starters, keep in mind that your colleague isn't getting under your skin on purpose. It's more likely that "they are reacting to things going on in their lives," says Fernandez. "You need to depersonalize the situation," he says. And look inward, McKee advises: "When someone is driving you crazy, it helps to ask yourself, What's causing me to react this way?" Your frustration "might not be about that person at all; it might be about you," she says. Perhaps your colleague even "reminds you of someone else you don't like." Having "self-awareness" and a deep "understanding of our own psychological makeup" strengthens your capacity for empathy, she adds. After all, cultivating compassion—both for yourself and others—is your primary objective.

Stay calm

Next, "lean in to your emotional self-control and will-power," McKee says. When your colleague shows up late, interrupts you, or is just being all-around obnoxious, you may feel a physiological reaction. "Recognize the clues that you're getting triggered. Maybe your breath quickens, or your palms start to sweat, or your temperature rises." Giving in to these symptoms risks *amygdala hijack*, where you lose access to the rational, thinking part of your brain. Instead, take a few deep breaths to "help you regulate your stress hormones and make it less likely that you'll engage in behavior that you won't be proud of later," she says. Keeping your "demeanor calm and open" puts you in a better frame of mind to conjure empathy for your colleague, Fernandez adds. "You're not caving, and you're not shutting down"; rather you're staying cool and collected and "maintaining awareness of the situation."

Be curious

There are two types of empathy: *cognitive empathy*— the ability to understand another person's perspective; and *emotional empathy*—the ability to feel what someone else feels. "Both of these tend to shut down when you feel annoyed or frustrated," McKee says. But you must fight against that.

- To summon cognitive empathy for an annoying colleague, McKee recommends generating theories that might explain "why this person says what he says, thinks what he thinks, and acts the way he acts. Unearth your curiosity," she says. Ask yourself: "What motivates this person? What excites and inspires him?" Go "beyond your own worldview" and reflect on "what may be in his cultural background, education, family situation, or day-to-day pressures that's causing him to behave this way." Remember: The goal here is to "understand this person's perspective," Fernandez adds. "It doesn't mean you have to adopt it, validate it, or agree with it, but you do have to acknowledge it."

- To muster emotional empathy for that colleague, "find something in them to care about,"

McKee says. One way to deal with someone who irritates you is to "picture that person as a six-year-old," she suggests. Remember that "they're only human." The hypotheses you generated to explain your colleague's behavior could be helpful here, too, according to Fernandez: "Maybe this person is stressed or under pressure, or maybe this person is just not having a very good day." You don't have to "become a psychologist and get into their childhood," but you do have to make an effort to experience "emotional resonance." The result is often, "I get it."

Focus on your similarities

Using both cognitive and emotional empathy, you must also try to "get to know the person" and deepen your "understanding of their perspective," McKee says. Rather than "focusing on your differences, look for the similarities" you share. "Start small," she advises. Perhaps you and your colleague have children the same age. Maybe your colleague lives in a neighborhood or town that you know intimately. Use those connections to strike up a conversation. If all else fails, "riff off an exchange you both seemed to find interesting in your last team meeting." Work often provides a neutral "common ground" for conversation, Fernandez says. Presumably both of you share a similar goal: "You want the organization to be successful."

Be kind

The fact is, "it's easier for you to be empathetic toward people you like because you give them the benefit of the doubt," McKee says. When dealing with someone you dislike, you often assume the worst, and that mindset shows up in your behavior. Try to short-circuit that reaction and "do or say something that's surprising and nice." Compliment the person on an idea they raised in a meeting or offer to help with a project. It shouldn't be forced, however. "It has to be authentic." Let's say, for instance, that your colleague arrives late—yet again—to your weekly team meeting. Don't complain or roll your eyes. Don't be passive-aggressive and quip, "Nice of you to join us." That may be your instinct, but fight it. Instead, McKee recommends something along the lines of, "Welcome. Get a cup of coffee before you sit down, and we'll get you up to speed." This type of generosity of spirit is good for you and your colleague. And remember, Fernandez says, empathy is a choice you can make in any scenario.

Have a (difficult) conversation

If you still find this particular colleague challenging, you might "have to have a conversation about how you work together," Fernandez acknowledges. But, he adds, "if you approach it through the lens of empathy, the conversation won't become charged." What's more, if you're "even-keeled and fair, your message will likely be received in a pretty good way." For instance, don't say, "You take up too much airtime." Instead, Fernandez suggests you try, "I'd love to figure out a way for us both to get our ideas out during the weekly team meeting." Don't lose sight of the fact that your colleague probably feels the same way about you. After all, McKee says, "if they drive you crazy, chances are you drive them crazy, too."

REBECCA KNIGHT is a senior correspondent at Insider covering careers and the workplace. Previously she was a freelance journalist and a lecturer at Wesleyan University. Her work has been published in the *New York Times*, *USA Today*, and the *Financial Times*.

Adapted from content posted on hbr.org,
April 23, 2018 (product #H04AM8).

9

Form Stronger, Longer-Lasting Connections

By Utkarsh Amitabh

Have you heard of Paul Erdős?[1] Erdős (pronounced "air-dish") was a quirky Jewish mathematician who could mentally, and rather quickly, calculate the number of seconds a person had lived by the age of four. *Time* magazine called him "the oddball's oddball."[2] He was known for showing up at people's doors at all hours, saying, "My mind is open."[3] What that meant was, "I'm ready to take on new mathematical challenges."

Over the course of his life, Erdős collaborated with more than 500 mathematicians. He also played "math matchmaker," introducing peers around the world to one another to advance mathematics research.[4]

These collaborations propelled the computing revolution and paved the way for modern search engines.

As it happens, Erdős himself wasn't the easiest of guests.[5] He couldn't make his bed or boil water for tea. He had very few clothes, so his hosts ended up doing his laundry. He also thought little of waking them in the middle of the night if he made a breakthrough in a problem they were trying to solve. Considering all this, you might find it puzzling that Paul Erdős was probably the most loved, most well-networked, and most talented mathematician of his time.[6]

You might be wondering, "How?"

I came across Erdős's work and philosophy while working on the mission statement for my company, Network Capital—a platform for career guidance and mentorship. I wanted to figure out a way to enable meaningful connections at scale. I was struggling with questions like, Why should my company exist? How can it become more than just another networking platform? The more I read about Erdős, the more intrigued I became. I found my answers in his philosophy, which focused on finding breakthrough solutions, making others successful, and not worrying about who gets credit.

The very nature of his collaborations taught me that networking can add value to others. Through his approach, I've learned how to form stronger, longer-lasting connections, and I encourage my community members to do the same when building out their professional networks. Here are three relationship-building strategies inspired by Erdős. Consider them as you expand your network and forge new connections at work.

Leave room for serendipity

Erdős believed in giving serendipity a chance in order to discover new areas for collaboration. He would enter conversations with an open heart and mind. Instead of jumping to a solution or being too eager to impress others with his knowledge, he would begin by asking thoughtful, open-ended questions. He truly engaged with the problem at hand and nudged others to open up about the precise problems they were struggling with. The result was that he not only helped his collaborators solve problems they were grappling with, but also empowered them to discover new ideas to work on.

Inspired by Erdős, I spend two hours every day speaking to Network Capital community members to discuss their career aspirations. The goal of these one-on-one, 20-minute coaching conversations is simply to understand what's going on in people's minds, what they're working on that's exciting them, or what they're struggling with. The first five minutes are allocated for an open-ended discussion and I often lead with, "So, what's on your mind?" It might seem a simple question, but people often talk about what's energizing them, what's bogging them down, or they simply state what they need me to weigh in on. This helps set the tone for the next 15 minutes, where

I try to find solutions that can best help them. Building the conversations this way lets me strike a healthy balance between structure and serendipity (great for new ideas!), and it has helped me strengthen my own relationships.

Pro tip: When meeting someone new or when having a first conversation with a client, start with an icebreaker—but reframe it. Instead of asking, "How's work going?" lead with, "What's exciting you these days?" This reframing can have a disproportionate impact on the depth and breadth of your discussions. While relationships take time to grow, they're unlikely to blossom into something meaningful if you focus all your conversations on utility.

Be clear about your goals

Erdős wasn't a man with hidden agendas, and he didn't mind healthy conflict. If he needed something, he would be clear about it. If he wanted to offer critical feedback, he would do so straight up. When he disagreed or debated with someone, they didn't doubt his intentions. His disagreements came from a place of curiosity, not judgment. And he was consistent with his behavior, irrespective of who he was collaborating with. This created a high-trust environment, which fostered deep collaboration.

Consistency compounds trust, and relationships thrive with consistency. Think about it: Would you trust someone who seems to have an ulterior motive to collaborate? In Erdős's case, by repeatedly showing up to help his collaborators, he demonstrated his commitment to making *them* successful.

Pro tip: When you're reaching out to someone for help, don't sandwich your ask, or worse, camouflage it. Be polite and give them an out, but also be straightforward. For instance, while writing my book, I reached out to several mentors for testimonials. I was direct in my ask and found it helpful to communicate the core point upfront: "I'd love for you to write a testimonial for my book. Coming from you, the recommendation would be very valuable and have a great impact on the readers. If you're unable to, I completely understand. No hard feelings." Most of the people I reached out to agreed.

Focus on adding value

Erdős's superpower was making others great. Instead of thinking about what he could get out of people, he collaborated with the intent of adding value to their lives—specifically by making their research more robust, nudging them to consider all possible scenarios, introducing them to other scientists, and working with them to fine-tune their research.

This attitude is best documented in what's called the *Erdős number*: the collaborative distance between

Erdős and another person.[7] In his lifetime, he had 509 direct collaborators. These were people with an Erdős number of one. People who have collaborated with his direct collaborators have an Erdős number of two (Albert Einstein among them).

One could reasonably argue that computing would have progressed at a slower pace had Erdős not built a social network of committed mathematicians who built off of each other's work. He was instrumental in the development of a branch of combinatorics known as the Ramsey theory, which other mathematicians and scientists have furthered. Today, it finds application in the field of quantum computing.

The beauty of this principle, of adding value and empowering others, is that it can be adopted by anyone. Adding value isn't dependent on seniority or your place in an organization. Whether you're speaking to your CEO or to an intern on your team, both have goals and dilemmas. Think about how you can help them face these challenges.

Pro tip: If you approach people with a generous and compassionate mindset, you, like Erdős, will likely be well-loved by your seniors, peers, and successors. Do you have information that can help someone design a better presentation? Can you connect them to the right person for a job? Are you willing to give feedback on their new idea? Even the tiniest gesture counts because people realize you're not just in it to get, but also to give.

I never met Erdős, but learning about his approach has shaped my outlook toward work and life. Empowering others to make the greatest impact through their careers is my mission. Every day, when I conclude my work, I ask myself how I can be a bit more like Erdős tomorrow. So far, it's served me well.

UTKARSH AMITABH is the founder and CEO of Network Capital, one of the world's largest mentorship platforms that empowers more than 7.5 million school students and 200,000 young professionals to build meaningful careers. An engineer by training, Utkarsh worked at Microsoft, studied moral philosophy at the University of Oxford, and earned his MBA from INSEAD where he was recognized as the Andy Burgess Scholar for Social Entrepreneurship.

Notes

1. László Babai and Joel Spencer, "Paul Erdős (1913–1996)," *Notices of the American Mathematical Society* 45, no. 1 (1998): 64–73; László Babai, Carl Pomerance, and Péter Vértesi, "The Mathematics of Paul Erdős," *Notices of the American Mathematical Society* 45, no. 1 (1998): 19–31.
2. Michael D. Lemonick, "Paul Erdős: The Oddball's Oddball," *Time*, March 29, 1999, https://content.time.com/time/subscriber/article/0,33009,990598,00.html.
3. Bruce Schechter, *My Brain Is Open: The Mathematical Journeys of Paul Erdős* (New York: Simon & Schuster, 2000).
4. Deborah Heiligman, *The Boy Who Loved Math: The Improbable Life of Paul Erdős* (New York: Roaring Brook Press, 2013).
5. Brian Rotman, "The Man Who Loved Only Numbers: The Story of Paul Erdős and the Search for Mathematical Truth," *London Review of Books*, September 17, 1998, https://brianrotman.wordpress.com/reviews-2/the-man

-who-loved-only-numbers-the-story-of-paul-erdos-and
-the-search-for-mathematical-truth/.

6. Adam Kucharski, "The Man Who Turned Coffee into
Theorems," *The Conversation*, July 22, 2013, https://
theconversation.com/the-man-who-turned-coffee-into
-theorems-16008.

7. The Erdös Number Project, https://sites.google.com/
oakland.edu/grossman/home/the-erdoes-number
-project.

Adapted from "3 Lessons in Collaboration and Networking
from Paul Erdos," on hbr.org, October 18, 2022.

10

Why You Need to Cultivate Your Sense of Wonder— Especially Now

By David P. Fessell and Karen Reivich

More than ever we need ways to refresh our energies, calm our anxieties, and nurture our well-being. One potentially powerful intervention is rarely talked about in the workplace: The cultivation of experiences of awe.[1] Like gratitude and curiosity, awe can leave us feeling inspired and energized. It's another tool in your tool kit, and it's now attracting increased attention due to more rigorous research.

As a physician and a psychologist, we've facilitated hundreds of resilience and well-being workshops, both before and during Covid, for the military, physicians, educators, law enforcement, and the business world. Helping participants to explore, experience, and recall moments of awe is one of the key scientifically-supported strategies we engage in during our workshops. It's been rewarding to see our participants benefit and take what they've learned back to their own organizations.

Awe and its benefits

In his book *Chatter*, University of Michigan psychologist Ethan Kross defines awe as, "the wonder we feel when we encounter something powerful that we can't easily explain." Often the things that bring us awe have an element of vastness and complexity.[2] Think of a starry night sky, an act of great kindness, or the beauty of something small and intricate. During your workday, the colors of the leaves outside your office or an act of sacrifice by a colleague could prompt a similar feeling—especially if you're attuned to it. Particularly in the United States and China, experiences of awe are frequently related to the virtuous behavior of others: an act of dedication, skill, or courage.[3]

Cultivating awe is especially important and helpful now as we renew our energy and make plans for a more hopeful future. That's because, beyond physical effects like tingling, goose bumps, and a lowered heart rate under stress, awe also affects us emotionally.[4] One experimental group, asked to draw pictures of themselves, actually drew themselves smaller in size after having an awe experience.[5] Such an effect has been termed *unselfing*.[6] This shift has big benefits: As you tap into something larger and your sense of self shrinks, so too do your worries and mental chatter. At the same time, your desire to connect with and help others increases.[7] People who experience awe also report higher levels of overall life satisfaction and well-being.[8]

Let's look more closely at the effects on stress and resilience. Experiences of awe are associated with lowered levels of reported stress; experimental research suggests that this may be a causal relationship: Awe can actively help reduce stress.[9] Research using functional magnetic resonance imaging (fMRI) has also shown that experiences of awe, such as watching awe-inspiring videos (compared to neutral or pleasant ones) decreases activity in the brain's default mode network (DMN), which is associated with self-focus and rumination.[10] The result is decreased mental chatter.[11]

Awe's benefits extend beyond stress relief, however. Research has shown that experiencing something bigger than us helps us transcend our frame of reference by expanding our mental models and stimulating new ways of thinking.[12] This can increase creativity and innovation and facilitate scientific thinking and ethical decision-making.[13]

It also helps us build relationships.[14] Though feeling awe frequently happens in solitude, it draws us out of ourselves and toward others, and inspires pro-social behavior like generosity and compassion.[15] Some scientists theorize that it's evolved to aid group cohesion and provide survival advantages.[16] For work groups, experiences of awe can lead to increased collaboration, team building, and social connection.[17]

There are many ways you can cultivate experiences of awe during your workday.

For individuals

If you can step away from your desk, a simple and powerful way to experience awe is to take an *awe walk*.[18] Take twenty minutes to wander and be curious and observe the everyday beauty around you, even in a familiar place like your yard or neighborhood. In our workshops, this instruction helps people to notice others, as well as places and things they might typically rush past—a bee flitting from flower to flower, for example. Afterward our participants report feeling inspired, calmer, and better able to focus.

Even better, take an awe-seeking walk in a natural landscape. Research shows that walks in nature, compared to urban environments, have a greater positive effect on our mood and well-being.[19] Nature is an immersive experience of growth and resilience; it can be a powerful source of wonder and awe. Nature's rhythms also remind us that we're a part of the natural world and that we too are enduring. A CEO of a Michigan technology company with whom one of us (David) has collaborated schedules frequent bike rides through a landscape of trees and water. Doing so, he feels a part of something larger than himself and boosts his energy and resilience.

If you can't step away from your desk, take advantage of the wonders at your fingertips on the web. Several studies have shown that videos can stimulate awe.[20] Perhaps you're inspired by award-winning documentaries such as *Free Solo*, *Planet Earth*, or the Oscar winner *My Octopus Teacher*. Let Amanda Gorman's "The Hill We Climb" give you goose bumps. The harmony and complexity of music can also elevate and inspire awe.[21] Create your own personal "awe playlist" of videos or music, and when you're feeling stuck spend a few minutes being drawn into what you're seeing and hearing. You can also invite moments of awe by asking the simple question, "What's beautiful here?"

Another option is to tune in to news sites that spread good news—acts of kindness, generosity, and perseverance.[22] Keep a file on your computer of stories of the goodness, benevolence, and decency of the human race. Tap it when you're feeling overwhelmed or depleted and want to be elevated. A simple story of one person making a difference can inspire others around the world.[23]

For managers and teams

If you're a manager, you can leverage the power of awe to help your team with its energy and resilience and to provide empathy and emotional support. Encourage your team members to share their awe playlists, and create opportunities to share experiences of awe by starting meetings with, "What took your breath away this week?" or "What made you glad you're on this planet?" (Contribute your own stories, too, and share their impact on you.) In work that one of us (Karen) did with the Oklahoma City Thunder, leaders asked team members to bring personal photos that sparked awe and gratitude. At a team meeting, the photos were projected, and then each person spoke about their photo and experience. Meanwhile, the health system where David works offers voluntary noontime resilience webinars featuring awe. Individuals from disparate departments who have never met come together and share stories of awe in small-group Zoom Rooms. The positive energy after each of these events is evident and elevating.

Managers should watch out for several potential missteps when creating awe experiences for their teams, however. First, what stimulates awe in one person can stimulate feelings of threat or danger in another—for example, if someone with a fear of heights is forced to look at a vertiginous view.[24] Know your team well enough to understand where to draw the line. Second, as you encourage your teams to experience awe, keep in mind that it's an addition and not a subtraction: Adding experiences of awe doesn't eliminate grief or anxiety; nor does it mitigate the need for teams to talk openly about the challenges they face and the support they need from leadership.[25] It's normal and healthy to experience a full range of emotions, especially in highly challenging times. It's imperative that managers offer as much compassion and understanding as they can muster. Finally, don't mistake intimidation for awe: We're not talking about developing a cult of power around yourself as a leader—a very different approach which can do more harm than good.

We spend much of our time at work trying to stake our claim and make our voices heard. It can feel counterintuitive to engage in something that might stimulate feelings of "smallness." But doing so through a positive experience of awe can, in the end, bring us that sense of grounding we're searching for, along with a multitude of benefits—such as energy, inspiration, and resilience—for ourselves and for our teams.

DAVID P. FESSELL is an executive coach, a faculty associate at the University of Michigan's Ross School of Business, and a retired University of Michigan professor of radiology. He writes and speaks on positive psychology and emotional intelligence and is a graduate of the Second City Improv Conservatory. KAREN REIVICH is Director of Resilience and Positive Psychology Training Programs at the University of Pennsylvania Positive Psychology Center. She is the coauthor of the books *The Resilience Factor* and *The Optimistic Child.*

Notes

1. Gretchen Reynolds, "An 'Awe Walk' Might Do Wonders for Your Well-Being," *New York Times*, October 1, 2020, https://www.nytimes.com/2020/09/30/well/

move/an-awe-walk-might-do-wonders-for-your-well
-being.html.

2. Yang Bai et al., "Awe, Daily Stress, and Elevated Life Satisfaction," *Journal of Personality and Social Psychology*
   120, no. 4 (2021), 837–860.

3. Yang Bai et al., "The Diminished Self, and Collective
   Engagement: Universals and Cultural Variations in the
   Small Self," *Journal of Personality and Social Psychol-
   ogy* 113, no. 2 (2017): 185–209.

4. Laura A. Maruskin, Todd M. Thrash, and Andrew J.
   Elliot, "The Chills as a Psychological Construct: Content
   Universe, Factor Structure, Affective Composition, Elicitors, Trait Antecedents, and Consequences," *Journal
   of Personality and Social Psychology* 103, no. 1 (2012):
   135–157; Bai et al., "Awe, Daily Stress, and Elevated Life
   Satisfaction."

5. Bai et al., "The Diminished Self, and Collective
   Engagement."

6. Michiel van Elk et al., "The Neural Correlates of the Awe
   Experience: Reduced Default Mode Network Activity
   During Feelings of Awe," *Human Brain Mapping* 40, no.
   12 (2019): 3561–3574.

7. Bai et al., "The Diminished Self, and Collective En-
   gagement"; Paul K. Piff et al., "Awe, the Small Self, and
   Prosocial Behavior," *Journal of Personality and Social
   Psychology* 108, no. 6 (2015): 883–899.

8. Melanie Rudd, Kathleen D. Vohs, and Jennifer Aaker,
   "Awe Expands People's Perception of Time, Alters

Decision Making, and Enhances Well-Being," *Psychological Science* 23, no. 10 (2012): 1130–1136.

9. Bai et al., "Awe, Daily Stress, and Elevated Life Satisfaction."

10. Van Elk et al., "The Neural Correlates of the Awe Experience."

11. Ethan Kross, *Chatter: The Voice in Our Head, Why It Matters, and How to Harness It* (New York: Penguin Random House, 2022).

12. Dacher Keltner and Jonathan Haidt, "Approaching Awe, a Moral, Spiritual, and Aesthetic Emotion," *Cognition and Emotion* 17, no. 2 (2003): 297–314; Michelle N. Shiota et al., "Beyond Happiness: Building a Science of Discrete Positive Emotions," *American Psychologist* 72, no. 7 (2017): 617–643; Barbara L. Fredrickson, "Chapter One—Positive Emotions Broaden and Build," *Advances in Experimental Social Psychology* 47 (2013): 1–53; Sara Gottlieb, Dacher Keltner, and Tania Lombrozo, "Awe as a Scientific Emotion," *Cognitive Science* 42, no. 6 (2018): 2081–2094.

13. Gottlieb, Keltner, and Lombrozo, "Awe as a Scientific Emotion"; Piff et al., "Awe, the Small Self, and Prosocial Behavior."

14. Fredrickson, "Chapter One—Positive Emotions Broaden and Build."

15. Shiota et al., "Beyond Happiness"; Piff et al., "Awe, the Small Self, and Prosocial Behavior."

16. Kross, *Chatter.*

17. Piff et al., "Awe, the Small Self, and Prosocial Behavior."

18. Virginia E. Sturm et al., "Big Smile, Small Self: Awe Walks Promote Prosocial Positive Emotions in Older Adults," *Emotion* 22, no. 5 (2022): 1044–1058.

19. Gregory N. Bratman et al., "Nature Experience Reduces Rumination and Subgenual Prefrontal Cortex Activation," *PNAS* 112, no. 28 (2015): 8567–8572; Jo Barton, Rachel Hine, and Jules Pretty, "The Health Benefits of Walking in Greenspaces of High Natural and Heritage Value," *Journal of Integrative Environmental Sciences* 6, no. 4 (2009): 261–278.

20. Rudd, Vohs, and Aaker, "Awe Expands People's Perception of Time"; Bai et al., "Awe, Daily Stress, and Elevated Life Satisfaction."

21. Michelle N. Shiota, Dacher Keltner, and Amanda Mossman, "The Nature of Awe: Elicitors, Appraisals, and Effects on Self-Concept," *Cognition and Emotion* 21, no. 5 (2007): 944–963.

22. Ari Howard, "Looking on the Bright Side: 7 Internet Sites to Find Positive Stories and News," AllConnect, October 17, 2020, https://www.allconnect.com/blog/good-news-websites.

23. Nicholas W. Eyrich, Robert E. Quinn, and David P. Fessell, "How One Person Can Change the Conscience of an Organization," hbr.org, December 27, 2019, https://hbr.org/2019/12/how-one-person-can-change-the-conscience-of-an-organization.

24. Kross, *Chatter.*

25. Elizabeth Bernstein, "How to Move Forward After Loss,"
Wall Street Journal, April 6, 2021, https://www.wsj
.com/articles/finding-meaning-as-we-grieve-a-year-of
-pandemic-loss-11617724799.

Adapted from content posted on hbr.org,
August 25, 2021 (product #H06JG2).

11

Four Phrases That Build a Culture of Curiosity

By Scott Shigeoka

Curiosity is a powerful practice to infuse into a company's culture. Research shows that managers are seen as more communal and friendly when they recognize their beliefs might be wrong.[1] Curiosity also reduces employee burnout and stress and is associated with higher levels of creativity and innovation.[2] When you build a culture of curiosity, people feel seen and heard—in essence, they feel they truly matter. This kind of positive organizational culture does wonders for employees' well-being, hiring top talent, retention rates, and productivity and fulfillment at work.

However, managers often get one major thing wrong about curiosity. They tend to limit its definition to a force to get information—something that powers our exploration or learning, for instance. Instead, we need to see curiosity as a more expansive practice. It's more than just an intellectual pursuit; it's a force for connection.

We need to move away from "shallow curiosity" and embrace "deep curiosity." This is the kind of curiosity that gives us more than data points or facts. It's a practice that centers on unearthing stories, values, experiences, and feelings. When conversations go beneath the surface in this way, curiosity can strengthen work relationships, foster a better understanding of yourself as a leader, and help you navigate conflict or anxiety in the office.

Curiosity is an exceptionally effective tool leaders have to guide diverse teams in our increasingly complex time of technological advancements and an ever-changing cultural pulse.

In my work writing *Seek: How Curiosity Can Transform Your Life and Change the World*; researching curiosity at the University of California, Berkeley,

Greater Good Science Center; and teaching ground-breaking courses at the University of Texas at Austin, I've uncovered four key statements that can intentionally build a curious culture in your workplace.

"I don't know."

Intellectual humility is a concept researchers define as, "the degree to which people recognize that their beliefs might be wrong."[3] Understanding the limitations of your mind and staying open to the wisdom of others is a critical tenet of curiosity. Many leaders fear saying, "I don't know," worrying that it makes them look ill-equipped for the job at hand. But research on intellectual humility shows that those who practice it are rarely perceived as less competent.[4] In fact, the opposite is true—they're seen as *more* competent and are viewed in a more positive light, as more communal and friendly. Team members prefer these traits in a leader as they are core ingredients to building trustworthiness.[5] Saying "I don't know" also indicates you aren't arrogant about having all the answers and you're open to the ideas of others.

It's important to follow up this statement with a course of action, however, because leaders still need to impart a culture of learning and growth, as well as a sense of confidence about the future. Asking a team something along the lines of, "But how might we learn more?" creates the kind of curiosity that encourages participation, collaboration, and problem-solving.

Practicing intellectual humility can also reduce anxiety in the workplace. An astonishing finding from one study found that intellectual humility was negatively associated with anxiety and positively associated with happiness and overall life satisfaction.[6]

"Tell me more."

For decades, psychologists John Gottman and Julie Schwartz Gottman have explored how we can strengthen our romantic relationships. They've found that a fundamental ingredient to longer, healthier, and happier marriages is responding to your partner's "bids" for your attention—a takeaway that can also be applied at work.

In other words, when your partner says, "I'm really enjoying this book," or "I saw the coolest thing on my walk," or "I had a tough day at work," respond with something more than just, "That's great" or "I'm sorry to hear that." Turn toward them with curiosity: "Tell me more about the book. What are you enjoying about it?" or "Tell me more about what you saw on your walk," or "Tell me more about what happened today." When you fail to respond to them meaningfully in these moments, you're missing a significant opportunity for connection.

At work, your team makes dozens of bids for your attention. They might say things like, "I'm learning a lot about generative AI, and it's really exciting," or "The timeline for this project feels a little too ambitious for me." When you miss these bids, you miss opportunities to maintain or strengthen your relationships with those you work with. Instead of moving on to the next agenda item, respond with, "Tell me more."

Strengthening our connections to others isn't just a feel-good human act. It's also good for business. Fostering a supportive environment can reduce employee burnout and stress, and positive workplace relationships are also associated with improved creativity and innovation.[7]

"I understand that you're more than your job."

There's so much going on in an employee's life, be it a family member's cancer diagnosis, a new baby, a dissolving marriage, moving to a new house, preparing for a volunteer fundraiser, or a set of challenges their child is experiencing at school. Employees are also impacted by what's happening in the world—for example, a hate crime in their community or the threat of a natural disaster that causes anxiety or fear.

When you ignore what's happening in employees' personal lives, you miss the chance to identify possible *work-life conflicts*. Researchers describe this phenomenon as the demands of someone's job (travel, irregular or late hours, occupational stress) clashing with those of the family (taking a child to swim class, attending an important event for a partner, caring for an elderly parent).[8] Research has found that unsolved work-life conflict has a consequence on employees' productivity and job performance, leads to higher turnover, and negatively affects psychological safety.[9]

Alleviating work-life conflict starts with simply acknowledging that we're all impacted by our personal lives and relationships and by world events. What goes on outside of work will, undoubtedly, ripple into one's professional life.

Creating organizational policies like parental and sick leave and providing mental health support or comprehensive health care alleviates some of the pains associated with work-life conflict. Acknowledging work-life conflict as a leader also cracks open the door of deep curiosity. Recognizing an employee's life outside of work allows your team to share more specifics about their home struggles (if they choose), in turn giving you a better idea of how to offer support. If you're successful, it doesn't just strengthen your relationship and improve their personal lives but also plays a role in the success of your organization.

"Who else?"

Contemporary work culture prioritizes answers over questions and is biased toward *who* has the answers. Fueled by assumptions, we often disenfranchise certain people from contributing their insights or solutions because we believe that only the developers—or leadership team or engineers—have anything of value to contribute.

The best leaders know that insights and solutions can come from unusual suspects who are rarely pulled to the brainstorming or decision-making tables. When I was bringing curiosity practices to the staff of Pixar Animation Studios, one animator shared a moment that shaped his views of how to develop films. The director pulled him and a group of Pixar team members into a room to review a scene from a forthcoming movie. When the director asked for feedback, one person raised their hand and said, "But I'm just an accountant." The director replied, "You were hired to work at Pixar because your voice, thoughts, and ideas matter. . . . You can make this film better."

After years of creating arguably the best animated movies the planet has ever seen, directors at Pixar realized that pulling feedback from a truly diverse group was going to give them more and better perspectives. By being curious about perspectives from those who didn't have the title "writer" or "animator" in their name, they were sourcing wisdom from a truly expansive and interesting group. They avoided homogenous groupthink.

No matter your company size or industry, you can bring this kind of curiosity to your organization by asking, "Who else might have unique insights or solutions to offer? Who else can we ask?" For a non-profit, it might be a diverse group of people who are benefiting from your work, like the communities you work alongside. For a small business, it might be your vendors or customers. Or maybe it's just walking into a different department in your own organization to find someone who can bring a new perspective, such as the accountant at Pixar. Brilliant insights and solutions can come from the most unlikely people—so long as you continue to question, "Who else?"

———————————

Incorporating these four phrases into your daily work will fast-track you, your team, and your organization to deep curiosity. But their impact doesn't stop there.

Research shows that when more of us model and see curiosity as valuable by using these kinds of phrases, it's more likely that others will adopt the practice, too.[10] Curiosity is contagious. The more you practice it in a visible way with your teams, the more likely it is they'll follow your lead—and that's how culture is built.

SCOTT SHIGEOKA is an internationally recognized curiosity expert, speaker, and the author of *Seek: How Curiosity Can Transform Your Life and Change the World.* He is known for translating research into strategies that promote positive well-being and connected relationships around the globe, including at the University of California, Berkeley, Greater Good Science Center, and through his popular courses at the University of Texas at Austin. He implements his curiosity practices with leaders in the public sector, *Fortune* 500 companies, Hollywood, media organizations, educational institutions, and small businesses.

Notes

1. Adam K. Fetterman et al., "On the Willingness to Admit Wrongness: Validation of a New Measure and an

Exploration of Its Correlates," *Personality and Individual Differences* 138 (2019): 193–202.

2. John R. B. Halbesleben and M. Ronald Buckley, "Burnout in Organizational Life," *Journal of Management* 30, no. 6 (2004): 859–879; Feiyuan Cao and Haomin Zhang, "Workplace Friendship, Psychological Safety and Innovative Behavior in China: A Moderated-Mediation Model," *Chinese Management Studies* 14, no. 3 (2020): 661–676.

3. Mark R. Leary et al., "Cognitive and Interpersonal Features of Intellectual Humility," *Personality and Social Psychology Bulletin* 43, no. 6 (2017): 793–813.

4. Fetterman et al., "On the Willingness to Admit Wrongness."

5. Daniel W. Newton et al., "Voice as a Signal of Human and Social Capital in Team Assembly Decisions," *Journal of Management* 48, no. 8 (2022): 2255–2285.

6. Neal Krause et al., "Humility, Stressful Life Events, and Psychological Well-Being: Findings from the Landmark Spirituality and Health Survey," *Journal of Positive Psychology* 11, no. 5 (2016): 499–510.

7. Halbesleben and Buckley, "Burnout in Organizational Life"; Cao and Zhang, "Workplace Friendship, Psychological Safety and Innovative Behavior in China."

8. Ellen Ernst Kossek and Kyung-Hee Lee, "Work-Family Conflict and Work-Life Conflict," *Business and Management* (2017), https://doi.org/10.1093/acrefore/9780190224851.013.52.

9. Sheena Johnson et al., "The Experience of Work-Related Stress Across Occupations," *Journal of Managerial Psychology* 20, no. 2 (2005): 178–187; Jeffrey H. Greenhaus and Nicholas J. Beutell, "Sources of Conflict Between Work and Family Roles," *Academy of Management Review* 10, no. 1 (1985): 76–88; Bojan Obrenovic et al., "Work-Family Conflict Impact on Psychological Safety and Psychological Well-Being: A Job Performance Model," *Frontiers in Psychology* 11 (2020), doi: 10.3389/fpsyg.2020.00475.

10. Rachit Dubey, Hermish Mehta, and Tania Lombrozo, "Curiosity Is Contagious: A Social Influence Intervention to Induce Curiosity," *Cognitive Science* 45, no. 2 (2021), doi: 10.1111/cogs.12937.

Adapted from content posted on hbr.org,
November 1, 2023 (product #H07VK8).

Index

abilities, reassessing, 44–45
Acker, Marsha, 87–99
agentic curiosity, 24
age of complexity, 53–54
Amitabh, Utkarsh, 113–125
amygdala, 80–81
amygdala hijack, 106
annoying people, developing
    empathy for, 101–111
anxiety, 23, 56, 146, 148
artificial intelligence (AI), 24
assumptions, 90–91
attention, bids for, 149–150
awe, 129–138
  benefits of, 130–133
  cultivating experiences of,
      133–138
  definition of, 130–131
  sharing experiences of, 135–138
awe walk, 133–134

barriers, to curiosity, 18–20
benefits
  of awe, 130–133

of curiosity, 3–4
Berlyne, Daniel, 4, 5
bids for attention, 149–150
blind spots, 42, 46
boredom, 22, 25–27
brain
  amygdala, 80–81, 106
  impact of awe on, 132
brainpower, 54–56
building curiosity, 15–31
burnout, 145, 150
bystands, 94–95

calmness, 105–106
Chamorro-Premuzic, Tomas,
    15–31, 51–61
coaching conversations,
    118–119
cognitive empathy,
    106–107
cognitive load, 55
Coleman, John, 63–76
collaboration, 45, 91, 117–123,
    148

colleagues
  conflict with, 12–13
  curiosity about, 107
  developing empathy for
      annoying, 101–111
  difficult conversations with,
      110–111
  idea sharing with, 20
  learning from, 37–38
  miscommunications with,
      87–99
  personal lives of, 150–152
  relationships with, 73–75
  similarities with, 108–109
collective curriculum, 39.
  See also learning
comfort zone, getting outside
    of, 24–25
communication
  breakdowns, 89
  face-to-face, 90
  miscommunications, 87–99
  See also conversations;
      listening
company culture, 145–155
compassion, 85, 104, 105, 132,
    137
complexity, 53–58, 130
compliments, 109–110
conflict, 146

  with colleagues, 12–13
  work-life, 151–152
connections
  forming stronger, 113–125
  making new, 37–38
  See also relationships
consistency, 119–120
continuous learning, 33–49
contributions, from diverse
    sources, 152–154
conversational intelligence,
    81–82
conversations, 80–81, 83–86,
    89, 90
  avoiding miscommunications
      in, 87–99
  coaching, 118–119
  curiosity in, 96–98
  deep, 146
  difficult, 110–111
  dynamic of, 93, 95
  feeling misunderstood in, 98
  "how" of, 92–93
  icebreakers in, 119
  internal narratives and, 90–91
  openness in, 117–119
  voicing observations in, 94–95
  "what" of, 92–93
  See also communication
cortisol, 80

coworkers. *See* colleagues
crafting, job, 66–68
craftsmanship, 68–71
creativity, 23–24, 132, 145, 150
culture of curiosity, phrases that
    build, 143–157
curiosity quotient (CQ), 57–58

daily routine, making changes
    in, 22–23
Deci, Edward, 5–6, 7
deep curiosity, 146
deep thinking, 21
default mode network (DMN),
    132
definition of curiosity, 17, 145–146
deprivation sensitivity, 7, 8, 12
development, at work, 35–39
difficult conversations, 110–111.
    See also conflict
difficult people, developing
    empathy for, 101–111
dimensions of curiosity, 4–13
Disabato, David J., 1–14
diversive curiosity, 5

Einstein, Albert, 58, 122
Ellis, Sarah, 33–49

emotional empathy, 106–108
emotional quotient (EQ), 56–57
emotional resonance, 108
emotional self-control, 105–106
empathy, 74, 85, 93
    for annoying people, 101–111
    cognitive, 106–107
    emotional, 106–108
employees
    burnout in, 145, 150
    personal lives of, 150–152
Erdős, Paul, 115–123
Erdős number, 121–122
experiences, novel, 22–25, 57
experimentation, 23–25, 38–39

face-to-face communication, 90
feedback
    asking for, 46
    from diverse sources, 153–154
Fernandez, Rich, 104–108,
    110–111
Fessell, David P., 127–142
five-dimensional model, 6–13

generative AI, 24
Glaser, Judith, 80
goals, 119–121

Goodman, Fallon R., 1–14
Gottman, John, 148–149
Gottman, Julie Schwartz,
    148–149

habits, 42–43
happiness, 73, 148
harnessing curiosity, 15–31
holdbacks, 42–43
humility, intellectual, 147–148

"I don't know" statements,
    147–148
information gap theory, 5
information overload, 53–54
innovation, 57, 132, 145, 150
insights, from diverse sources,
    152–154
intellectual humility, 147–148
intelligence quotient (IQ),
    54–56
interests, building on your,
    20–22
internal narratives, 90–91
interpersonal skills, 56–57, 90
intrinsic motivation, 6, 20–21, 69

job crafting, 66–68
jobs, learning at, 35–39

job skills, 18, 39, 56–57
joyous exploration, 8–9, 7–12

Kantor, David, 89–90, 94
Kashdan, Todd B., 1–14
Kaur, Manbir, 77–86
kindness, 109–110
Knight, Rebecca, 101–111
Kross, Ethan, 130

leaders, intellectual humility in,
    147–148
learn-fast log, 38–39
learning, 17–18
  continuous, 33–49
  from errors, 25
  extrinsic-based, 26
  from others, 37–38
  through experimentation,
    38–39
limitations, understanding your,
    147–148
listening
  attitudes of, 81–82
  to cocreate, 82
  defensive, 81
  for intention, 83
  to judge, 82
  neurochemistry of, 80–81, 82
  skills, 77–86

tips for, 83–86
See also communication
Loewenstein, George, 5

managers
  culture of curiosity and,
    145–155
  intellectual humility in,
    147–148
McKee, Annie, 101–102,
  105–111
McKnight, Patrick, 7
meaningful work, 63–76
memory, working, 55–56
mental ability, 54–56
mental chatter, 131, 132
miscommunications, avoiding,
  87–99. *See also* conversations
motivation, intrinsic, 6, 20–21

nature, walking in, 133–134
Naughton, Carl, 1–14
neurochemistry, of listening,
  80–81, 82
neutral observations, 94–95
novel experiences, 22–25, 57

observations, voicing your,
  94–95

open-ended questions, 85–86,
  118
organizational culture, 145–155
organizational policies, 151–152
others
  adding value to, 121–123
  focusing on similarities with,
    108–109
  learning from, 37–38
  perspective of, 46, 90–91, 94,
    107–109, 153–154
overstimulation, 5
oxytocin, 81

perfection, quest for, 68–69
PERMA framework, 73
personal lives, 150–152
perspective, of others, 46,
  90–91, 94, 107–109,
  153–154
Pixar, 153–154
points of view
  alternative, 41
  See also perspective
positive relationships, 73–75,
  150
problem-solving, 65, 118, 148
professional relationships
  curiosity and, 146, 149–150
  investing in positive, 73–75
  listening and, 77–86

propelling questions, 43–44
pro-social behavior, 132–133

questions
  asking "why," 20
  "even better," 46
  open-ended, 85–86, 118
  prioritizing answers over,
    152–153
  propelling, 43–44
  "what," 20–22

reading the room, 91–98
reflection, 104–105
Reivich, Karen, 127–142
relationships
  adding value in, 121–123
  building stronger, 117–123,
    132–133
  listening and, 77–86
  positive, 73–75, 150
  romantic, 148–149
  trust-building in, 119–121
  work, 146, 149–150
  See also professional
    relationships
relearning, 44–47
Renner, Britta, 6, 7
research on curiosity, 4–13

resilience, 47, 129–132, 134
routines, changing your, 22–23

self-awareness, 105
self-driven exploration, 26
self-evaluation, 67
self-improvement, 69
Seligman, Martin, 73
sensation seeking, 6
serendipity, 24, 117–119
service to others, 71–73
shallow curiosity, 146
Shigeoka, Scott, 143–157
Silvia, Paul, 11
similarities, focusing on, 108–109
skills swaps, 39
small successes, 47
social curiosity, 7, 9, 12–13
soft skills, 56–57
specific curiosity, 5
strengths solving, 45–46
stress, 23, 56, 131–132, 145, 150
stress hormones, 80, 106
stress tolerance, 9, 11–12
structural dynamics, 90
success
  ability to learn for, 35–36
  IQ and, 54
  professional, 65
  small, 47

supportive environment,
149–150

tasks, switching, 25–26
technological change, 53–54,
146
"Tell me more" statements,
148–150
thrill seeking, 10, 11
trades, 68–69
trust, 81, 119–121, 148
Tupper, Helen, 33–49

understimulation, 4
unlearning, 40–44
unselfing, 131

value, adding, 121–123
videos, awe-inspiring, 134–135
volunteering, 71

well-being, 131, 145
"what" questions, 20–22
"white spaces," 21
"why" questions, 20
wonder, sense of, 127–142
work
    avoiding miscommunications
        at, 87–99
    connecting to service, 71–73
    as craft, 68–71
    learning at, 35–39
    lives outside of, 150–152
    meaningful, 63–76
    positive relationships at,
        73–75
    relationships, 146, 149–150
work crafting, 66–68
working memory, 55–56
work-life conflicts, 151–152
workplace curiosity, 12–13, 19–20

Zuckerman, Marvin, 6, 11

How to be human at work.

HBR's Emotional Intelligence Series features smart, essential reading on the human side of professional life from the pages of *Harvard Business Review*. Each book in the series offers uplifting stories, practical advice, and research from leading experts on how to tend to our emotional well-being at work.

Harvard Business Review Emotional Intelligence Series

Available in paperback or ebook format. The specially priced six-volume set includes:

- Mindfulness
- Resilience
- Influence and Persuasion
- Authentic Leadership
- Happiness
- Empathy